GO!

GO!

An inspirational guide to getting outside and challenging yourself

TOBIAS MEWS

Quarto is the authority on a wide range of topics.

Quarto educates, entertains and enriches the lives of our readers – enthusiasts and lovers of hands-on living.

www.QuartoKnows.com

First published in Great Britain
2017 by Aurum Press Ltd
74–77 White Lion Street
Islington
London N1 9PF

Photography by © James Carnegie
Page 73 © David Pearson/Alamy Stock Photo
Pages 103–107 by kind courtesy of Cedar.com/*High Life*

A catalogue record for this book is available from the British Library.

ISBN 978 1 78131 640 5
Ebook ISBN 978 1 78131 685 6

10 9 8 7 6 5 4 3 2 1
2021 2020 2019 2018 2017

Typeset in 10/14pt Amasis by carrdesignstudio.com
Printed in China

FSC
www.fsc.org
MIX
Paper from
responsible sources
FSC® C104723

To my long-suffering beloved wife, best friend
and adventure sidekick, Zayne.
Thank you for so many happy memories.
And here's to lots more.

Author's note

1) **Don't be reckless**. By this I mean, use your common sense and don't take unnecessary risks. If deep down you think it's a bad idea, it probably is. Always check local laws to make sure where you are running or cycling is safe and open to the public.

2) **Know your limitations**. Some of the challenges in this book can be fairly vigorous, so before you go Everesting or racing vertical kilometres, just make sure you're up to the task and have sought any medical advice if you need to do so.

1) **Be safe**. If you're racing from peak to peak or wild swimming in remote lakes, it's a good idea to do a quick risk assessment. Ask yourself questions like, 'If I slip and hurt myself, where will I get help from?' 'Do I have cell phone signal up in the mountains?' One of the reasons why it's good to do these challenges with friends is that if one of you has a problem, the other can go get help.

2) **Have fun**. Whilst it's important to feel that sense of achievement at beating your personal best, or scaling new peaks, it is not more important than staying safe, staying within the law and being sensitive to local customs. The premise for the ideas in this book are to get you outside, ideally with your friends, and challenging yourself. But don't take yourself too seriously – its about having fun too!

Contents

#GoRaceItYourself

Introduction

I love to race. From the nervous excitement I experience on the start line, followed by a rush of adrenaline as I step outside the boundaries of my self-imposed limitations, right through to those juicy endorphins as I reach the finish. I love the whole experience. And having completed more than 200 races of almost every distance and discipline across five continents, all described in my first book, *50 Races to Run Before You Die*, it's fair to say I'm addicted.

In the closing chapter of *50 Races*, I describe a fell race: over the course of five days and virtually self-supported, I ran 200 miles across the mountainous spine of Wales, with nothing but a map and compass to guide me. I so enjoyed that feeling of autonomy, working out what route to take, the mixture of adrenaline and fear I experienced as I crawled along the treacherous Crib Goch, and then the feeling of arriving at the finish, set in the ruins of an ancient castle – and I wondered how I could top this. I had waited three years for the race, and if I wanted to repeat the experience, I would have to wait again.

Then it struck me: I didn't have to wait. I didn't need to worry about not getting a slot in a race before it sells out. I didn't even need to enter another race to get that outdoor fix. I could simply organise my own challenge, as I had been doing on and off for over a decade. If a race is similar to going for a special meal in a restaurant, then what I needed to do for the other days of the week was to learn how to cook for myself. Ultimately, the preparation and planning of an adventure is half the fun.

And so began a personal quest to create a series of Race It Yourself challenges. Using the knowledge and skills I picked up from my time in the army, I began to analyse my environment, looking for lakes to swim in, mountains to run up, trains to race against or castles to cycle between. Rather than look for the easiest route, I'd look for the most difficult. Essentially, I was turning the ordinary into something extraordinary.

After moving my family from London to the French Pyrenees, I found myself not only entering the odd race, but also racing funiculars with my wife, creating SwimRun routes in the mountains, collecting cols to enter archaic French cycling clubs, bagging peaks, and even creating time trial routes between twinned towns. And in all of these endeavours, there were no entry fees to find. I just needed to grab a map and get outside.

The best way to think of this book is as a series of recipes for adventure – or templates for athletic challenges where, just like in a race, the emphasis is on performance. They're not meant to replace organised races, but rather to complement them, allowing you in an act of spontaneity to get outside and challenge yourself.

Some of the ideas, like Everesting, are based on existing challenges. Others, like Extreme Twinning, I've created from scratch. But the one thing that binds them all is the fact that you can do these challenges anywhere in the world. And in most cases, at any time. And for that reason, the book has been divided up into three sections: **Midweek Madness**, **Wacky Weekends** and **Long-Term Burners**.

HOW TO USE THIS BOOK

The ten challenges you'll find in **Midweek Madness** are ones that you can slip into your everyday routine. They're designed to be fun and easy to plan but still take you out of your comfort zone. Some ideas, like racing a funicular, might take only a few minutes, whereas others, such as a Five to Nine adventure race, will see you racing up to 16 hours through the night.

But if you're looking for something a bit more challenging, something that requires training and gives you those all-important bragging rights, then flip over to the **Wacky Weekends** section. This is where you'll find athletic challenges that will push you further. You could be trying to run around a mountain before sunset, racing a mountain train, or creating your own Tri-It-Yourself triathlon.

And then there are the **Long-Term Burners**. These are challenges that you slowly tick off over time or do in your holidays. You might spend your weekends collecting cols with the aim of becoming an Officer of the Ordre des Cols Durs. At the other extreme, you might plan a week-long bikepacking expedition following a river from its source to sea.

STATS

As in a recipe book, the graphics at the top of each chapter give an overview of what's involved: what type of challenge it is; how long it takes to research and prepare for (excluding the training required, because this is personal); how long it will take to complete, whether it's good to do with friends/family; and how difficult it is. Moreover, because we live in a social media age where we're defined by hashtags, I've provided one to use when sharing your challenge. #GoRaceItYourself

KIT

I've also provided a rudimentary kit list. As I don't want to teach you to suck eggs – like suggesting you bring a puncture repair kit for a bikepacking adventure – it's not exhaustive. Moreover, a lot depends upon the weather, climate and the nature of the terrain. But you'll quickly realise that most of what you need can be whittled down to a dozen or more essential bits of kit – from running shoes and a bike, to a map and GPS tracking device.

RULES

If you've ever harboured a desire to complete a Bob Graham Round, take on an Everesting challenge or set a Fastest Known Time on an historic national trail, there are always rules. And so, where possible I've given some guidelines for you to follow. But since these are templates for challenges you'll create, it's up to you to set the rules for others to follow.

BE SOCIAL

Just like going out for a meal, you should not necessarily do these challenges alone. Sitting down with a group of friends around your kitchen table, with a glass of wine as you pore over a map, trying to figure out how long it will take to run around an island in a day, all

before the last flight home (see Day Flight Run, page 102) – those moments are precious. Or discovering more about your city by seeing how many commemorative plaques you can find within 60 minutes (see page 10). It's so much more fun with friends.

And lastly, in each chapter I've included several examples to get you started as well as suggestions of similar challenges that you might like. There are loads more options, which you'll find on www.hardastrails.com.

So grab some mates, pick an adventure, buy a map, get outside and start challenging yourself. There is a world to explore. All you need is a pinch of imagination and a dash of courage.

Gear

BIKE

Choosing a bike can be an exciting process. But with so many different types, from full suspension mountain and gravel bikes to carbon road bikes and to oversized fat bikes, it can also be daunting. Sadly, there is no one bike that does them all, but a few get pretty close.

For bikepacking, many argue that the best bike is the one you have in your garage. The general consensus is: the less suspension, the less that can go wrong, but if that's all you have, don't let it stop you from using it. Where touring bikes are used for long-haul trips, laden with heavy panniers, here we're more

focused on ultra-lightweight cycle touring using bikepacking luggage such as seat bags that fit under your saddle, frame bags that distribute the weight, and handlebar bags useful for holding your sleeping bag or mat.

WETSUIT

If you're not a fan of the cold, then a wetsuit is going to be your friend. You don't necessarily need the most expensive, just make sure it's a good fit and allows for decent movement in the water.

For a SwimRun (see Wild at Heart, page 78), take an old wetsuit and cut off the legs at the knees and potentially the arms (from the elbow). If you do not already have one, buy one second-hand. A rash vest can also be a good investment. If you're swimming in Alpine lakes or the sea, that extra layer can be a godsend.

GPS

The GPS device is one of the single most brilliant bits of technology ever invented. And although it has made navigation considerably easier, it shouldn't replace your map. It's simply an aid to help find your way.

There are two types that you'll want to have a look at.

• For running

Use a GPS watch, such as a Suunto Ambit or Garmin Fenix. These have a long battery life.

• For cycling

A running watch will suffice for tracking. If you want mapping, then you'll need a dedicated bike GPS.

RUNNING SHOES

Most of us have a pair of road shoes – which are what you'll use for some of the challenges in the Midweek Madness section. But for most of the other challenges in the book, you'll need to invest in a pair of trail shoes.

The type of shoe very much depends upon the terrain. For urban trail challenges like Hidden Waters or Day Flight Run, where you'll

be moving between the road and trail, you'll need a hybrid trail shoe where the outsole isn't too aggressive and provides enough cushioning.

But for a fastpacking challenge, you'll need something a little more substantial. Lightweight, minimalist shoes won't be ideal if you're planning a multiday Hut to Hut challenge. Rather, look for a shoe that's not too heavy, but robust enough to handle anything you chuck at it.

BACKPACK

The secret to choosing the right pack for your activity is to find one that's just a tiny bit smaller than what you think you need. The less space you have, the less likely you are to try to carry the kitchen sink with you.

Many outdoor brands sell a running specific hydration pack, often equipped with soft lightweight flasks that slot into a pocket at the front or one with a bladder that sits along your back. These lightweight packs also have pockets designed for keys, food and a mobile phone, as well as a larger compartment (5–10 litres) at the rear for putting your essentials – a waterproof jacket, spare top, etc. These types of pack are ideal for many of the challenges in the Midweek Madness and Wacky Weekends sections.

But for longer, fastpacking-style, multi-stage challenges, like Hut to Hut or Peak to Peak, which can last up to a week or more, you'll need something larger – closer to 15–25 litres. You'll also need a dry bag to keep your kit protected from the elements.

PAPER MAPS

If there was one piece of kit, crucial to every activity in this book, it's a paper map. They hold the key to adventure. The best maps are the 1:25,000, simply for the level of detail they give you, often highlighting routes that a 1:50,000 won't show. But ultimately any map is better than no map, so make sure you always pack one, along with a compass.

FOOD

Your choice of food is going to be a personal one. But since we're all about moving fast and light, think more along the lines of cereal bars, dried fruit and nuts, energy bars and gels. But don't forget to use what's available to you. There's nothing stopping you from stocking up en route at supermarkets, cafés and restaurants.

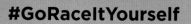

#GoRaceItYourself

MIDWEEK MADNESS

ADVENTURE ANY TIME

Many of us live a time-poor existence, rushing from home to work and back again.

If you're anything like me, what I love is that feeling of spontaneity – just doing a challenge whenever the need takes you.

Consequently, the challenges you'll find in this section are all feasible during the week. What's more, with the exception of the Vertical Kilometre and perhaps the Five to Nine, they can very easily be adapted to an urban environment. The shortest challenge, Race the Funicular, might take you a few minutes depending upon your nemesis. The longest is the Five to Nine, and if you eke it out to the bitter end, it will take 16 hours.

Whichever you choose, the challenges are designed to fit in and around your working day.

You don't even need much kit. If you're in possession of a pair of running shoes, you can complete every single challenge in this section.

The beauty about these Midweek Madness pop-up races is that you can slip them into your holiday just as easily as you might swig on a latte. If you happen to be passing by a funicular, why not just stop and see if you can beat it? The most important thing to remember is, anything is possible. These are just templates to get you started. And remember, it's no good keeping it to yourself. Tell your friends about it, and challenge them to see if they can beat your time.

60 Minutes

PREPARATION TIME — **1 HOUR**

ADVENTURE TIME — **1 HOUR**

Yes

1 2 3 4 5
DIFFICULTY

 ## CONCEPT

As creatures of habit, we like to know how long something will take. But in contrast to a race, which is often limited by distance, this orienteering-style challenge is about squeezing in as much as you can within 60 minutes, all while exploring your local neighbourhood.

✏ RULES

1. Your time is limited to 60 minutes.

2. You decide how you're going to spend your time – 'collecting' monuments, running as far as you can, juggling while running, or even running between Starbucks cafés.

🧭 KIT

- Smartphone with 3G connection
- Running shoes
- GPS watch to track route and keep track of time

METHOD

For many of us, especially those with children, the concept of time can have no meaning. Sometimes it feels as if we've stepped through a wormhole in which hours pass in the same way that minutes do. Which is why you'll appreciate this challenge. With 1,440 minutes in a 24-hour time period, there's no reason you can't use 60 Minutes of your day for something new – whether it's before or after work or even during your lunch break. And what's more, it's ideal to do with friends and family.

And the key to all of this is a map. That folded piece of paper puts us all on a level playing field where fitness levels can be offset by the ability to navigate. As the saying goes, 'It doesn't matter how fast you are if you're going in the wrong direction'.

The first stage is to look at what's around you and see if there's a pattern. Are you in a city with lots of churches, like Naples? Or perhaps you live in a place such as Madrid, where there are dozens of statues? Essentially it's a case of joining the dots and seeing if a pattern emerges.

When I lived in London, I was intrigued by the Blue Plaques attached to the side of various

homes and buildings. On my runs, I'd stop to read them, learning that a famous poet, author, politician or soldier had lived in that very house. If I had my phone with me, I'd take a photo, to remind me to learn more about the person when I got home. 'I wonder how many Blue Plaques I can visit in an hour?' I thought to myself.

For the amateur historians among us, the commemorative plaques offer endless possibilities in which to learn something new about your area. In Paris you could learn about its remarkable history by looking for the Histoire de Paris oar-shaped plaques, designed by Phillipe Starck. Should you happen to be in Rome, you could try to visit as many marble wall plaques as possible. These were a trend from the late nineteenth century and, like London's Blue Plaques, they commemorate the lives of interesting people who have lived in that property. Or if you're passing through Berlin, there are more than five thousand cobblestone-sized memorials, called Stolpersteine (literally 'stumbling stones'), each laid on pavements outside the homes of 'a single victim of Nazism'.

After a bit of research, I found a map that showed where many of the Blue Plaques are situated. But with more than two thousand to choose from, I decided to limit myself to a postcode, which in my case was London's

SW11. Of course it could be an arrondissement, canton, or any other administrative area with a boundary.

You're not just limited to historical plaques. In a bid to generate interest in a major film being released, some production companies work alongside tourism bodies by laying out temporary statues around a city. For example, when the irrepressible Paddington Bear was appearing in cinemas, more than fifty Paddington statues were scattered around London. The same thing happened for the films celebrating Shaun the Sheep and the Big Friendly Giant, making it the perfect excuse to drag your family with you on an adventure. So keep an eye on the big screen – you never know what will happen.

I've been running around my local borough for many years, although I've been a slave to the same old routes. Armed with a map and

my GPS-enabled smartphone as a backup, I now find myself darting down roads that were otherwise invisible to me. From quaint cobblestone mews streets to ordinary-looking high streets hiding interesting people, I start to see these streets with fresh eyes. With some of the eminent residents dating back three to four hundred years, my imagination runs wild as I try to picture what it must have been like back then. So much has changed.

I hardly notice the minutes pass, until the clock on my phone indicates my time is up. I've 'collected' 26 plaques, covered 11 kilometres, discovered areas I hitherto haven't known existed and in the process learned so much about my area, including the fact that I live less than a mile from a former prime minister. But the most salient fact I learned is that the only thing we're limited by is our imagination.

A FEW EXAMPLES
- TO -
GET YOU STARTED

Church steeples

Padlocks in Rome

Blue Plaques in London

Tube stations

Wall plaques in Rome

Starck Oars in Paris

The Stolpersteine of Berlin

How many bridges can you run across in Amsterdam?

Race the Funicular

 PREPARATION TIME **1 HOUR**

 ADVENTURE TIME **1 HOUR**

 Yes

 1 **2** 3 4 5 **DIFFICULTY**

 ## CONCEPT

There are hundreds of funiculars spread across Europe. Ordinary people take them to save having to climb up the hill. The challenge here is to see if you can run up the hill quicker than the funicular.

RULES

1. The race starts the moment the funicular starts to move and finishes when it comes to a complete standstill.

KIT

- Running shoes
- GPS watch

METHOD

If you're of the athletic outdoors type, it's possible you've not taken a funicular before, dismissing the rather odd-looking contraption on the basis that unless you're carrying heavy shopping or a troublesome two-year-old, you'd rather walk up the hill than take the 'cheat' version.

Indeed, it's not exactly a word that falls off the tongue, but funiculars can be found everywhere. In America, where they're known as incline railways, they're commonly seen taking alpine skiers up the slopes. But in Europe, where the funicular was born back in the fifteenth century, they are mostly found in cities, where they were used to move heavy stuff up and down steep hillsides – making them brilliantly accessible to anyone looking for a quick urban challenge.

'Do you want to walk or take the easy option?' my wife asks me, as we admire the funicular in Pau, on the edge of the French Pyrenees. I crane my neck upwards and follow the tracks leading directly up to its destination high above us, before bringing my gaze back to where the funicular operator was looking at us expectantly. It's then that I notice a path snaking its way up

TOP TIPS?

This challenge is great to involve your family and friends, so encourage them to take the funicular while you run.

✓

**IF YOU LIKE THE SOUND
OF THIS, THEN TRY:**

Race the Commute

Race a Mountain Train

Day Flight Run

the hill, crisscrossing underneath the rail tracks and hopefully arriving at the same point as the funicular stops. 'I've got an idea,' I say with a wink. 'You take the funicular and I'll race you to the top.'

I had no idea if it would work, and later research would prove that not all funiculars are worthy race opponents, with some disappearing into tunnels, others through gaps in a rock face or, like those found in Istanbul, almost entirely underground – making it difficult to run beside (unless you take the above ground option). The key to making this challenge work is if there's a path running alongside the line – or at least one in proximity.

My wife gives me one of those looks that says: 'You're mad,' and then enters the carriage while my daughter giggles with delight. Most funiculars, especially the old-fashioned type, operate in a similar fashion to an elevator, being pulled up by a cable while a second carriage balances the weight as it descends. With departures about every three minutes, the doors to the funicular remain open while the upper and lower operators wait for passengers. It's simple,

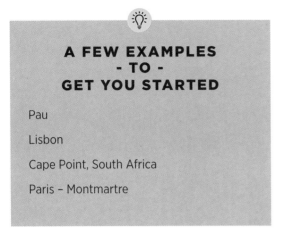

A FEW EXAMPLES
- TO -
GET YOU STARTED

Pau

Lisbon

Cape Point, South Africa

Paris – Montmartre

but clever. And best of all, many of them, like this one, are free.

The operator repeatedly looks at me, as I seem to be loitering for no good reason, until eventually I tell him my plan. At first he's puzzled, but then with a wry smile he steps into the driving seat, gives me a wave while twisting a few knobs and ringing a bell, and sets the funicular in motion – my cue to start running.

Of course, my enthusiasm is greater than my fitness and I go off way too fast, causing my calf muscles to course with lactic acid from being on my toes. Perhaps this wasn't going to be so easy after all, I thought to myself as I huffed and puffed my way up the hill. It might only be 30 metres of elevation, but when that's crammed into such a short distance, it's a challenge not to succumb to walking.

High above me, I can hear my wife shouting: 'Go, Tobias,' as I edge further up the hillside. Pumping my arms like a steam train, I ignore the pain in my legs, and make the final turn that will

bring me out to the top – just as the funicular is starting to arrive. Luckily, it slows down enough in the final few metres for me to take the win, with rapturous applause from my wife and some of the other passengers. I've done it, but in the back of my mind, I know with a little training, could go much faster…

Dare to Dash

USING A COMMON SET OF DICE, LET LUCK DETERMINE WHAT ACTIVITIES YOU DO

PREPARATION TIME
1 HOUR

ADVENTURE TIME
1-4 HOURS

Moderate

1 **2** 3 4 5
DIFFICULTY

 ## CONCEPT

Although we love keeping fit and healthy, following a training plan can become a little repetitive. Sometimes, we need to spice things up a bit, throw caution to the wind and try something new. Dare to Dash essentially involves leaving your daily or weekly plan to chance. A simple roll of the die to determine your fate... Where will it take you?

✍ RULES

1. Whatever number you roll, you have 24 hours to follow through with it.

2. You decide what the numbers mean and what activity you do.

3. There are no second rolls.

🧭 KIT

- Dice
- Running shoes

METHOD

Even the fittest and most experienced athletes can find it difficult to remain motivated. Perhaps you've just completed your latest marathon, and you're searching for a new goal. Or maybe, you've fallen out of love with running or cycling. Either way, trying to squeeze in your training to an already busy day when you're lacking focus can be hard work. As a fallback position, most of us end up doing the same run we always do. The one we've done for the past four years.

Having fallen into this rut myself, I found myself listening to an American podcast where some guys on a road trip rolled a die to determine what they'd do that day. Four of the options indicated their direction (north, east, south or west); the fifth option was staying put; and the last, to cross the nearest state border. They ended up rolling 300,000 miles of adventures. It got me thinking: what if we could apply the same technique to our daily training?

When the first dice were created 8,000 years ago, they weren't playing board games; rather, the dice were made of knucklebones (astragali) and were used by religious shamans to interpret the signs from the gods. A thousand years later, the Mesopotamians squared them off to the

TOP TIPS?

While this chapter mainly focuses on running, Dare to Dash applies just as well to swimmers and cyclists.

If doing it on your own, to begin with don't be too ambitious or make some of the challenges too difficult.

✓

IF YOU LIKE THE SOUND OF THIS, THEN TRY:

60 Minutes

YoYo Peaks

7 in 7

six-sided cubes we have today, though it wasn't until 1300BC that the pips were added to the sides.

Stealing some dice from my board games, I began to come up with a series of options that corresponded with each number. And to make things even more interesting, I found dice of a different colour to denote a different approach to running. Red, for instance, was for adventure; white for distance; and blue for speed work. I'd then dip my hand in a bag, pull out one die (red for adventure, say) and roll it to see where it would take me.

At first, I'd do this when I was ready to go for a run, but then I'd end up faffing about trying to find a route, etc. So instead, I'd either roll it the night before or first thing in the morning, which would give me enough time to make a plan and, where possible, to rope in some friends to join me for an evening game of chance.

Of course, doing this by yourself is all very well, but I quickly realised it gets interesting only when you do it with friends. Your ability to get creative increases dramatically as you come up with somewhat silly ideas that none of you

necessarily want to do (run ten times up and down the tallest skyscraper you can find), but it adds another dimension to the game and turns a potentially boring training session into a midweek adventure run.

By the end of my first week, this simple process of a roll of the dice had given me a new lease of life. I'd raced buses, climbed skyscrapers, taken a random train to the first stop it comes to and then run back, and even run a marathon (see Boundaries Run, on page 52). For the first time in a while, I was having fun again. Who knows where the dice will take you next?

A FEW EXAMPLES
- TO -
GET YOU STARTED

Adventure

1 = Race a bus, train or boat (see Race the Commute, page 34)

2 = Run to the highest three points in your area

3 = Take a bus or train somewhere and run back

4 = Do a night-time trail run

5 = Run to a new pub/bar/café and indulge in cake

6 = Do an urban triathlon

For a daily plan:

1 = Draw new routes and create GPS art

2 = Running every path in the park

3 = Take a rest day

4 = Run Pi (3.141592) – adding up the accumulative numbers for the corresponding day of the week. For example, if it's Thursday, the fourth day of the week, run 9 miles (3+1+4+1)

5 = Run to and from work

6 = Go tech-free (no GPS, no music, no watch, no phone)

For a distance-related plan:

1 = 1 mile

2 = 5k

3 = 10k

4 = a half-marathon

5 = marathon

6 = Stay put and eat cake

Run the Bridges

RUN THE STRETCH OF THE RIVER CROSSING EACH BRIDGE – CHOOSING YOUR LENGTH

PREPARATION TIME
1 HOUR

ADVENTURE TIME
1 HOUR

No

DIFFICULTY

 ## CONCEPT

If you live in a city, especially a flattish one like London, Paris, New York or Rome, there's a high chance you might struggle to get elevation into your runs.

The idea is to run a stretch of river, anything from 5 kilometres to an ultra (a distance further than a marathon), crossing each of the bridges so that you run on alternate sides of the river.

RULES

1. You must only cross bridges that are accessible to the public.

KIT

- Running shoes
- GPS watch

METHOD

What does almost every capital city have in common? The answer is they have a river running through them! In fact, it's not just the capitals but almost every major city. And where there's a river, there's almost guaranteed to be a bridge – which makes the Run the Bridges challenge extremely accessible to anyone living in a city.

Your first plan of action is to decide how far you want to run, because in some cities you could be out there for a while. There are 37 bridges crossing the Seine in Paris and at least 35 in London.

The great thing about bridges – apart from the fact that many are stunning examples of architecture both ancient and modern – is they provide you with a simple route and it's almost impossible to get lost. However, on the flip side, as I've discovered through bitter experience, some bridges (railway bridges in particular) don't allow for pedestrians, so you might have to adjust your route slightly. Equally, you'll find that it's not always possible to stay as close to the river as you'd like, due perhaps to a private gated development, a government building or even a port.

Which is why the next stage, using any form of mapping tool – whether that be MapMyRun, Strava or even Google Maps – is to get online and plot a route. You'll quickly find bridges you can and can't cross, thanks to the likes of Google Street View and, more importantly, the advent of the 'global heatmap' created by Strava Labs, which shows the heat signature of every single running and cycling activity created by its members.

As an ultra runner, I was initially tempted to run all of the River Thames' bridges, but with limited time and a pregnant wife at home, I decided to turn this challenge into my 'midweek, middle-distance run'. So I plotted a 23-kilometre route through the centre of London, from my home near Putney to the iconic Tower Bridge, taking in 16 historic

TOP TIPS?

When planning your route, global heat maps, as used by Strava and Garmin Connect, will make your life a lot easier.

IF YOU LIKE THE SOUND OF THIS, THEN TRY:

Source to Sea

Hidden Waters

Sea to Summit

Race the Commute

bridges. From there I could simply jump on the Tube to take me back home.

Although I'd run along the Thames many times, I'd never tried to cross every bridge before. So, before I left my home, I did a tiny bit of research on each of the bridges I'd be crossing – just to make my run feel more interesting. I wasn't after breaking any speed records, but rather to do a decent long run and simultaneously learn something new.

Just like running between lamp posts, running between bridges is the perfect way to practise fartlek training (fast running mixed with slow running). You can pick up the pace either between the bridges or, if you want a greater challenge, as you go over them. Indeed, it's thanks to running the New York Marathon that I discovered bridges are the equivalent of hills. They may not look like much, but they subtly go up towards the middle. Which means that even in Amsterdam – one of the flattest cities in Europe and home to the Amstel river, 165 canals and more than 1,200 bridges – you can get at least a little bit of elevation gain.

Besides the fact that there's something extremely calming about running along a river,

arguably the main artery of a city, the riverside is also where you'll find more mansions, posh hotels, museums, government buildings and monuments than you can shake an energy gel at. When I'm not running over a bridge, I find myself gazing in awe at iconic postcard-worthy landmarks, reminding me that I've yet to visit many of them. Then, of course, I bump into the hordes of perplexed tourists wielding cameras and maps.

As I weave around the final bend of the river, I can spot in the distance the mammoth structure known as Tower Bridge. Knowing that I have no more than five bridges left, I up my speed, zigzagging my way along the Thames like a drunken runner, all the while feeling a sense of delirious delight in my little adventure across London.

In the space of 23 kilometres, I've crossed 16 historic bridges, done some fartlek and hill work, seen dozens of iconic landmarks. All I have to do now is get home. Isn't there a bus or train I can race, I wonder.

A FEW EXAMPLES - TO - GET YOU STARTED

Amsterdam bridges

Rome bridges along the Tiber

Paris bridges along the Seine

London bridges along the Thames

Race the Commute

PREPARATION TIME **1 HOUR**

ADVENTURE TIME **1–1½ HOURS**

 Yes

 1 2 3 4 5 **DIFFICULTY**

CONCEPT

The idea of this challenge is to encourage you to think outside of the box and turn the ordinary into something extraordinary – to race your commute. Everyone has to get to work – most of us by public transport – so it's the perfect routine to make into a challenge.

RULES

1. The race starts at the point the public transport leaves and finishes at its destination.

KIT

- GPS watch
- Smartphone
- Running shoes

METHOD

Unless you have the pleasure of working from home, commuting is a necessary evil if you're to get to your place of work. Millions of us gear ourselves up to squeeze into an underground train and then avoid eye contact with our fellow passengers. Millions more put up with sitting in bumper-to-bumper traffic, wondering whether it would have been quicker on the Tube, with some muttering: 'I could get there faster on foot.' There is, of course, only one way to find out.

There are five principal means of public transport: the underground train, passenger boats, overland trains, trams and buses. When choosing your commuting rival, much will depend upon your fitness levels, what public transport is available and, of course, how sweaty you want to be on arrival, whether at work or home. Moreover, each requires slightly different tactics, but like some of the other Man vs Machine challenges in this book, the crucial element you'll need is a risk of failure. It's simply not a race if either you or the machine is significantly quicker than the other.

Luckily, every form of public transport has a timetable with scheduled stops, a route plan and the all-important departure and arrival times. You can make it as easy or difficult as you like. For instance, you can follow the exact route of the bus or train, choose various 'checkpoints' (key bus stops, Tube stations, etc.), or simply go as directly as your paths allow.

After looking at the boat timetable and then playing around with various options, I selected a route from home near Putney in southwest London to the Thames Clipper's final stop, 6.6 miles and 44 minutes away at Blackfriars in the City. And apart from a little shortcut at the start that knocked off a bend in the river, almost all of the route followed a traffic-free footpath, giving me ample opportunity to keep an eye on my nautical competition. All I needed to do was run an average of 6:40 minutes per mile. It would be tough, but doable.

Having opted for an early morning race before work, I recruited some friends to join me. Some volunteered to take the coffee and paper route aboard the boat while another opted to cycle using the local bike-sharing scheme. For my friend Matt and me, there was only one option – to race it on foot.

We had no ambitions of setting a Fastest Known Time, but simply to see if it was possible to beat the boat. Ordinarily, we would expect a boat, or any other form of public transport for that matter, to be much quicker than us humans. But I made a discovery during my battle with a hundred-year-old steam train in the iconic Race the Train event in Wales: trains, just like boats and any other form of public transport, need to stop to let off passengers – giving the chasing commuter a chance to gain advantage.

However, just as boats have to slow down, so do we. Running in rush hour can sometimes be just as frustrating as driving. It requires us not only to dodge the occasional commuter walking to the Tube station, naturally oblivious to our quest, but also to stop occasionally at traffic lights and road crossings. However, every opportunity to catch one's breath is a welcome reprieve.

And after just 40 minutes of running, our breathing is getting progressively heavy as Matt and I both cast a glance over our shoulder towards the river on our right. Not far behind, the sun is glistening on the sleek boat that seems to be chasing us. We feel we can hear laughter from its suited and booted passengers, probably saying, 'They have no hope in hell.' Feeling ever more determined, the two of us pick up the pace, our gaze focused on the large pier beneath the bridge some 500 metres in front of us. It's going to be tight, but we might just beat it.

'We thought we were going to beat you,' my friends say as they disembark from the boat, to

find us standing by the pier, somewhat sweaty, but with enormous grins on our faces. By chance, we arrived at the pier with one minute to spare, and interestingly enough, at the same time as my friend who'd opted to cycle, but who'd been hampered by traffic lights.

'Who's up for racing a bus?' someone says, as we walk up the pier gangway, and on our way to work.

A FEW EXAMPLES
- TO -
GET YOU STARTED

Race the No 100 Bus across the centre of Berlin

Race the Batobus along the River Seine in Paris

Race the No 19 Tram across Rome, from the Piazza del Risorgimento to the Piazza dei Gerani

Urban Tri

CREATE AN URBAN TRIATHLON ON YOUR DOORSTEP

PREPARATION TIME
1 HOUR

ADVENTURE TIME
1-2 HOURS

 **Moderate**

1 **2** 3 4 5
DIFFICULTY

 ## CONCEPT

If you live in a city or town, there's a very good chance you have everything you need to complete your own 'urban triathlon'. All you need is somewhere to swim, a bike hire scheme and a footpath or park to run around.

✒ RULES

1. Swimming facilities should be available to the general public (or through membership, where necessary).

2. There should be a bike hire location available.

3. The run can be completed on or off road – as long as it's not on private land inaccessible to the general public.

⊘ KIT

- Goggles
- Swim cap
- Wetsuit (optional)
- Running shoes
- Triathlon suit or similar
- GPS watch

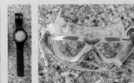

🦶 METHOD

Triathlon has been one of the fastest growing sports in the world for the last four years. But with ever increasing entry fees, the need to buy a bike, a wetsuit and various bits of triathlon paraphernalia, not to mention the cost of travelling to the event, finding accommodation – well, the bills start to add up, and you may not be entirely sure you want to make the investment until you've tried it out. Moreover, if there's one element to put the uninitiated off mass-participation triathlon events as favoured by novices, it's the thought of getting punched and kicked at the start of the swim in the melee of arms and legs.

But if you're looking for a multi-sport challenge that you can fit in and around your working week and which won't cost you more than a pint of beer, then read on.

The biggest hurdle to planning a triathlon is finding somewhere to swim. But you don't need to look far. I chose the 40-acre Serpentine in central London on the basis that if it was a venue good enough for the London 2012 Olympic Games and a World ITU triathlon event, it's certainly good enough for an early morning 'urban triathlon' dip before work. But I could have chosen any other public swimming pool, river, lake or even, if given the option, the sea.

Having figured out where to swim, the next crucial element in making this challenge feasible, fun and as free as possible is the bike. Of course, I could have used my own. But not everyone has one, so instead I chose to take advantage of my city's bike-sharing scheme. And with more than 600 cities around the world offering one, from Paris's Velib to Milan's BikeMi, we're all on a level playing field.

Having located a Boris Bike docking station near the lido, I planned a fun cycle route – which isn't difficult when you've got a myriad

of dedicated cycle routes like the ones scattered around Hyde Park. And with time being of the essence, I followed the Sprint distance triathlon template of a 750m swim, a 20km bike and a 5km run.

And so, at 7 a.m. on Tuesday morning, I set off. As the water hits my face, I feel a giddy sense of exhilaration, putting into touch any drowsiness. In those brief seconds spent staring into the cold and murky depths of the Serpentine Lido, I don't feel any fear or self-doubt, common at the start of a race. On the contrary, despite

the fact that I am by myself apart from one or two seasonal swimmers, I feel more content as I surface for air than I have in the countless triathlons I've done in the past.

Feeling a mixture of exhilaration and exhaustion, I exit the water, collect my small backpack and run towards my de facto transition area, simultaneously casting hungry glances at the nearby café serving warm cups of coffee. That's my reward, I tell myself. I get a couple of strange looks from tourists who've stopped to watch me struggle out of my wetsuit to reveal, like a poor man's version of Superman, a Lycra trisuit in which I've stashed my credit card. Hands still cold, I can't help but chuckle to myself as I fumble to remember my pin number!

It's not often you see someone in a trisuit and riding a Boris Bike – a steel contraption as aerodynamic as the proverbial brick and a hundred times as heavy to boot – but I don't care. In fact, it all adds to the comedy value and makes the entire experience much more fun.

To add to the challenge, if I want to avoid paying another £2 for the bike hire, I have only

30 minutes to squeeze in as much as possible of the required 20km – which even top cyclists might struggle to achieve. But 16 kilometres later I return the bike to the docking station, none the poorer but feeling a tiny bit wobbly on the feet. Then I begin my run, following the footpath dedicated to the memory of Princess Diana.

As I run through central London, passing commuters, heads bowed towards their phones, I fall a little bit more in love with the city. There's so much to see and appreciate, if only you take the opportunity to look. It doesn't matter where you live, there's no excuse not to get outside and do more. And what better way than an urban triathlon before (or after) work!

A FEW EXAMPLES
- TO -
GET YOU STARTED

Pau – Swim in the Olympic outdoor pool, cycle around the city on its bike-sharing scheme, race up and down the Boulevard des Pyrénées

London – Swim the Serpentine, take a Boris bike around Hyde Park, then run the Princess Diana Memorial path

Hidden Waters

TRACE AND RACE THE HIDDEN RIVERS OF YOUR CITY

1 HOUR — PREPARATION TIME

1-3 HOURS — ADVENTURE TIME

Moderate

1 2 3 4 5

DIFFICULTY

CONCEPT

If you were asked to name a river running through a city, most of us can come up with an obvious name – the Seine in Paris or the Tiber of Rome. But how often can you name a second, third or fourth river? The chances are, you can't. Although almost every major city was built around a river, there are also a plethora of hidden rivers, now long forgotten and unbeknown to many. But if you go looking for them, you'll find they still pass right under our feet – leaving an invisible trail to follow.

RULES

1. You should follow the river as faithfully as possible.

2. The route you choose must be accessible to all and sundry.

KIT

- Running shoes
- GPS
- Map

METHOD

There is something exciting about discovering the secret side to a city. Often, you think you know your backyard and then, out of the blue, you discover something new, something that takes you aback. In my case, it was the assortment of hidden rivers that so many cities have, but which no one knows about.

'This can't be it,' I say to myself in disbelief. In front of me, and barely deep enough to get my feet wet, is a somewhat muddy and sorrowful-looking spring. But according to my research, this unremarkable trickle of water in a corner of Hampstead Heath marks one of two sources of the River Fleet, one of London's most famous subterranean rivers.

If you were to step back in history to the time of the Romans, the Fleet was a major river in its own right. But over the course of centuries, and not helped by the Industrial Revolution, pollution has got the better of it and nowadays much of this quintessential river is underground. But as I traced its watery remains through the streets of London, I could still feel its heartbeat beneath my feet.

In this day and age, when Google Earth

has mapped the world, allowing us to explore mountains and deserts without even leaving the comfort of our sofas, it's easy to see why urban exploration seems so exciting. Hidden catacombs, bomb shelters, disused underground stations, sewage tunnels, derelict factories and, of course, hidden rivers – all are undetectable to satellites but begging to be explored. The snag is that unless it's a tourist attraction, much of it is illegal. But there's nothing illegal about the Hidden Waters challenge, as it's all above ground, if you'll excuse the pun.

✓

IF YOU LIKE THE SOUND OF THIS, THEN TRY:

Boundaries Run

Monopoly Marathons

Trail Time Travelling

You could say this challenge is a mashup of urban exploration and running. Rather than running away from security guards and the police, it's about following hidden rivers that lie under our feet – an almost invisible route that will be obvious only to those who've taken the time to discover their original path. For me, someone who loves looking at maps, to track down the history behind the Fleet felt more like a treasure hunt than simply plotting a route.

So, your first port of call is to get online and Google 'lost', 'subterranean' or 'underground' rivers in your local city. There's a good chance it will send you to the Wikipedia minefield – which often has tons of random lists and information. But if you strike lucky, you might find some bloggers who've done some of the grunt work for you, perhaps helpfully providing you with a map, tracing its path.

Equally, when I was researching the Fleet in my local library, I found copies of ancient maps, books and etchings from a time lost to memory. And there's a very good chance you'll find the same for your own city.

It's worth noting that many of Europe's underground rivers have now become sewers,

such as Paris's Bièvre. So where there's a sewage tunnel, there's a manhole cover – once again, giving you a clue as to what's beneath you.

Map in hand, I leave the leafy pastures of Hampstead Heath, and follow quaint streets, ancient churches and many of London's most iconic buildings. I find snippets of its watery remains with the odd street sign or an old pub sign with a river on it – just little things, but all adding to the mystery as I try to imagine what

the Fleet must have been like 1,000 years ago, when so much of it was above ground.

And then I stop my watch, my journey coming to a close as I meet with the Fleet's big brother – the River Thames. It has taken me just over an hour to run 6 kilometres – not a Personal Best, but definitely one of the most fun runs I've had the pleasure of doing in my own city. And with dozens more to choose from, I'm spoiled for choice as to my next hidden river!

A FEW EXAMPLES
- TO -
GET YOU STARTED

The Bièvre, in Paris

The Fleet, in London

The Saw Mill, in New York

Boundaries Run

RUN AROUND THE ADMINISTRATIVE EDGE OF YOUR LOCAL BOROUGH, TOWN OR POSTCODE

PREPARATION TIME
1 HOUR

ADVENTURE TIME
1-5 HOURS

Yes

1 2 **3** 4 5
DIFFICULTY

💡 CONCEPT

With 90 per cent of the world's population living in an urban environment, there's a good chance you live in an administrative borough. But do you know where the borough starts and finishes? The idea of the Boundaries Run is to run as close as possible around the perimeter of your boundary or postcode, creating a permanent race route for those living there.

☑ RULES

1. The route needs to follow the boundary line as closely as possible and should avoid private land not accessible to others.

2. If you're the first to create a Boundaries Run, then you determine the start and finish point – which must be used by others.

🧭 KIT

- Smartphone
- GPS
- Running shoes
- Running pack (e.g. Salomon S-Lab vest) with hydration
- Food

METHOD

It's fair to say, we're all creatures of habit. How many of us run the same routes over and over again – the well-trodden paths that take a set amount of time, pass familiar landmarks and generally speaking don't require any thought or imagination? It's easy to get stuck in a running rut, even if you are following a training programme.

Which is how I came to be sitting at my kitchen table staring at an A–Z map of London. Bored of running around my local park, I was searching for new paths, commons or parks to run in, anything to escape the monotony of my regular evening run. And then, by chance, I noticed a blue line tracing around my local borough of Wandsworth. It snaked along disused rivers, around parks and through housing estates – a continuous line of purple marking the boundary of one of London's thirty-two boroughs, just as you'd find in any other city. It was a lot larger than I'd imagined.

In fact, it doesn't matter where you live in the world, I can say with almost 100 per cent certainty that you'll live in an administrative zone – a borough, county or commune. At the very least, you'll probably have a postcode that you could run around. Some, of course, will be larger than others – and perhaps more suitable to cycling around (see Perimeter Bicycling, page 194) – but the idea is that you should be able to complete the run during the week, whether it's before work or after. Or perhaps even fit it into your Five to Nine (see page 64).

Grabbing a pen with excitement, I started to annotate the map, marking up a route that followed the blue line as closely as possible. As I closed the final section of the circular loop, I was visibly grinning like the proverbial Cheshire Cat – I was on the verge of a new adventure and yet I'd never be further than between 5 and 7 miles from my home!

In this generation of Google Maps, you may not be confident following a paper map, so it's a good idea to plot your route onto Strava or similar – just to get that warm and fuzzy feeling you're on track. It will also allow you to figure out how far you'll be running – which in my case I learned would be just over a marathon.

But watch out! Because when it comes to following a city map, or indeed your smartphone, you need to allow for a certain amount of what

I call 'the faff factor'. Somehow, as soon as you step off your familiar route and start following a GPS or map, everything takes longer – whether it's stopping to figure out where you are, reaching a dead end, pausing to take photos, waiting at traffic lights – it all adds up.

Luckily, for a challenge of this nature, you don't need much – a small running vest to store some water, a smartphone, money and some spare food. I decide also to pack a head torch – just in case I'm out a little later than expected.

I don't have a particular time in mind when I leave my home – although I do warn my wife that we'll be eating out for dinner – as I'll be starting and finishing at one of our local pubs. I simply run at a pace I know I can sustain for 26-odd miles. As I follow the blue line on my map, occasionally checking my phone to ensure I am on track, I feel as if I'm on a treasure hunt. I run down streets that I've hitherto ignored,

IF YOU LIKE THE SOUND OF THIS, THEN TRY:

Perimeter Bicycling

Monopoly Marathons

Tri-It-Yourself

Run the Bridges

Trail Time Travelling

A FEW EXAMPLES - TO - GET YOU STARTED

Run the 16th Arrondissement of Paris (17km, around an area 15.62km²)

Wandsworth Borough of London (43km, around an area 34.62km²)

Kreuzberg district in Berlin (17km route, around an area 10.41km²)

across small parks frequented by dog walkers but invisible to tourists, along a tributary of the Thames that's been in use since Roman times, past interesting-looking shops and cafés that I've never known about – it really is fun.

In a normal race you'd have to survive on gels or what's available on the course, but in this instance, I simply stop at convenience stores whenever I'm hungry or thirsty. In how many marathons do you get to eat ice cream? And thanks to it being summer, it's still light by the time I've completed the loop, some 4½ hours after I've set off. It would have been even more of a challenge in the depths of winter.

'Was it fun?' my wife asks me, as I gave her a sweaty hug in the pub, where she's waiting for me. I hesitate for about a second before saying: 'It's the best marathon I've never had to pay for.'

Vertical Kilometre

TO ASCEND 1000M IN AS SHORT AMOUNT OF TIME AS POSSIBLE

PREPARATION TIME
1 HOUR

ADVENTURE TIME
1-5 HOURS

Moderate

1 2 3 **4** 5
DIFFICULTY

CONCEPT

While most races are about distance, this is all about height – hence the name Vertical Kilometre. In the world of sky running, it means you 'run' (as best you can) up a mountain until you have reached 1,000 metres of vertical gain in the shortest distance possible – and certainly not exceeding five kilometres in length. As you can appreciate, it's hard work.

🖊 RULES

1. The race starts at the bottom of the mountain and finishes at the top. You can make it more difficult by adding in the descent.

🚫 KIT

- Bike
- Helmet
- Waterproof jacket
- Running shoes
- Running pack
- Puncture repair kit
- Bike padlock
- GPS watch

🐾 METHOD

'Are you ready?' I ask my friend Reuben, who is making some last-minute adjustments to the mountain bike I've lent him.

'Of course I am,' he answers before pedalling off to a nearby hotel, our notional start point. If you're going to create a challenge built around a mountain, it's good idea to start and finish at a hotel/café/pub, giving you something to look forward to when you reach the finish.

It was by accident that I found myself on a bike, rather than skis. I'd arrived in Scotland's Cairngorm National Park to go ski touring up the Cairngorm Massif, the UK's sixth highest mountain. But despite being December, there was no snow, so I needed to find a new challenge.

After a decent amount of staring at 1:25,000 map, I realised to my delight that it was almost a vertical kilometre from the nearby town of Aviemore, sitting at 228 metres above sea level, to the summit of the munro (mountains in Scotland over 3000ft) at an altitude of 1,245 metres. Even better, there was a choice of routes to get up there, with a mountain bike path handrailing the road – all adding to the excitement and making it perfect for recruiting friends to join you.

Ordinarily Vertical Kilometres are done on foot, but there's absolutely no reason why you can't do it on a bicycle and on foot. Indeed, what makes this particular challenge great is that there are a ton of options to suit your fitness level and/or your appetite for adventure.

And even if you live in a country or region that isn't particularly blessed with mountains and therefore somewhat vertically challenged, you can still find creative ways to get 1,000 metres in, for example doing a mini Everesting challenge (see page 138).

We set off at a gentle pace, simply enjoying being outside. Luckily, the first part of the route is easy going, allowing us to ride side by side before Reuben splits off the main road onto the dedicated bike trail running alongside.

Even though we are on different types of bike, we can't help but egg each other on as we catch glimpses of each other through the foliage separating us.

TOP TIPS?

Try looking for ski stations, as these make the perfect venue for a Vertical Kilometre.

If you can't find a mountain 1,000 metres high (or more), try creating a route that has 1,000 metres of elevation gain – even if it's running up the same hill thirty times.

But as soon as we pass a rather magical-looking crystal lake, things start to get punchy, the road taking a decidedly upward slant. It isn't just the ascent that is punishing, but the sudden headwind and rain blowing into us we grunt our way up the mountain. But as so many would agree, it wouldn't be challenging if there weren't a bit of pain before the gain of reaching the top.

Having climbed the best part of 450 metres in around 15 kilometres of cycling, just getting to the ski station is enough of a challenge, but Stage 2 awaits us. The funicular railway would certainly be the quickest way to get to there. And when we are told about the wind-chill factor of -8°C at the summit, to add to the 40mph winds, it's very tempting to sack off the run and jump on. But that would be cheating.

After locking up our bikes, we swap helmets for our running packs and immediately set off up the gravel path. Within moments my calves feel like they want to explode. I lived in London for a large part of my life, and hills didn't feature much in my daily running routine.

✓ IF YOU LIKE THE SOUND OF THIS, THEN TRY:

Sea to Summit

Everesting

Peak Bagging

Peak to Peak

Race a Mountain Train

Race the Funicular

But 35 minutes later, after a decent amount of huffing and puffing, we reach the Top Station. Ideally, we'd have carried on to the summit, but the wind was now pretty vicious, so we decided to stop for lunch instead!

After a hearty meal, we even manage an added bonus: to slip in a Race the Funicular challenge, running down the mountain in less than 10 minutes and beating the funicular by a whisker.

As we get on our bikes to make our way back to our cars in Aviemore, we feel a huge sense of achievement. We may not have got to ski, but as we freewheel down the mountain, we cannot care less! We've just done an awesome multi-sport Vertical Kilometre with a little amuse-bouche at the end.

Five to Nine

HOW FAR CAN YOU GO DURING YOUR 16-HOUR BREAK BETWEEN YOUR 9 TO 5?

PREPARATION TIME
3 HOURS

ADVENTURE TIME
16 HOURS

No

1 2 3 4 5
DIFFICULTY

 CONCEPT

For the majority of people, the working day starts at nine and finishes at five – which leaves 16 hours to squeeze in an overnight adventure challenge. This can be absolutely anything of your choosing – cycling from A to B and back again, running to your highest summit or even kayaking across a lake – as long as you're back at your desk by 9 a.m. the following morning.

 RULES

1. You are limited to 16 hours to complete this challenge.

2. Trains or buses are permitted if they help you get to your destination, as long as they aren't the principle means of transport – i.e. you still need to do something epic.

 KIT

- Running Pack (10-15 litre)
- GPS
- Smartphone
- Bivouac sack (AKA sleeping equipment)
- Sleeping bag/ sleeping liner
- Head torch and spare batteries
- Shoes

⬛ METHOD

As I ride along the ancient footpath at night, the beam from my cycle light reflecting off the eyes of creatures hiding in the foliage, I feel an almost giddy rush of adrenaline. On the one hand I'm nervous – the task I've set myself of mountain biking the 120 kilometres from my home in the foothills of the Pyrenees to Hendaye, on the Atlantic coast, is fairly daunting. On the other hand, I'm excited. I've done plenty of night-time escapades before, almost all on a weekend, but never on a Tuesday night.

Although I love living in the mountains, I sometimes long for the sea. So I decided that I'd try and squeeze in an overnight mountain bike ride with the aim of arriving on the beach at some point in the middle of the night, camping out and then catching the train back home in time to be at my desk at 9 a.m. I'm half tempted to run the route and perhaps will do so on another occasion, but for now, I'm keen to get on my mountain bike and head to the sea.

Earlier that day, I'd hardly been able to contain my excitement, constantly casting glances at the clock on the study wall, counting down the minutes to 5 p.m. 'Not long now,'

I would say to myself. My 9 to 5 working day was about to finish and I couldn't wait to make the most of the remaining 16 hours of pure adventure bliss that awaited me.

Doing a pop-up adventure race on a work night takes some mental arithmetic to get your head round. After a hard day's work, most of us want to put our feet up, have a drink and get a good night's rest in preparation for the following morning's onslaught of emails and meetings. But with a little planning and an open mind, there's nothing stopping you and your friends

TOP TIPS?

Make sure you have a decent head torch or cycle light. And don't forget to bring spare batteries.

Depending upon where you are, it can get cold at night, so bring spare warm clothes.

There's no perfect time to do a Five to Nine, but the eve of your birthday or the summer/winter solstice are great excuses.

from having a proper midweek adventure every now and again and, most importantly, doing one that pushes you out of your comfort zone.

The hardest part of a Five to Nine adventure is deciding what to do. Alastair Humphreys, the man behind the excellent 'microadventures' concept, would suggest finding a decent hill, bivouacking out, having a nice breakfast and then getting back home in time for work. But since this book is all about pushing the boundaries of our self-imposed limitations, I'm all for something with a bit of jeopardy.

You don't want to arrive late for work, but try to do something where you're pushed to continue, even when you're tired. Sometimes we need a tight deadline to bring out the most in us.

As my journey into the night continues, I begin to battle with the dreaded sleep monsters – imaginary creatures that appear on the trail when you're tired and ready to sleep. I stop by the path, and sit against a gate to grab ten minutes of shut-eye – sometimes the only way to put these monsters at bay.

By the time I reach the outskirts of Hendaye, it's still very much dark, but I'm grateful for the street lights to guide me through the final stretches. It's so quiet I can almost hear the sea, even though it's still 1km away. I make my way to the sandy beach, feeling the euphoria of having reached my destination, before getting my bivouac shelter out and falling into a satisfying sleep. Not for long, though, as I have an early morning train to catch to take me home.

I arrive back home just in time to feed our daughter, grab a quick shower and get to my desk with minutes to spare. It's time to face a new day, but boy was the last one a goody!

A FEW EXAMPLES
- TO -
GET YOU STARTED

Cycle from Pau to Bayonne, take the train back

Take a train out and run back

#GoRaceItYourself

WACKY WEEKENDS
THE GETAWAY CHALLENGE

At last, it's the weekend. That glorious moment, which for many is the carrot dangling at the end of the proverbial stick. It's our chance to get some mates together, escape the city, get outside and, most importantly, challenge ourselves while having an adventure. And with 64 hours to kill, from 5 p.m. on Friday before we've got to be back at work at 9 a.m. on Monday, there is no end of possibilities.

The really fun bit, the element I like most about these challenges, is the brainstorming process, often done over a bottle of wine, in which you come up with that barmy idea that will get the grey matter firing on all cylinders. In short, what I'm proposing is that you become your own race director.

You'll find that the challenges in this section are a step up from the Midweek Madness – a little bit more difficult and therefore requiring a little more preparation but nevertheless still allowing room for spontaneity. Some of the challenges,

like Everesting or YoYo Peaks, require a high level of fitness and aren't the sort of thing to attempt on a whim – unless you like punishing yourself. But that's where you set a date in the diary and use some of the other challenges in the book as preparation for those events.

Can it be done? Am I fast or strong enough? Will I make it in time? Where will I stock up on food? How do I get back? Think of these ideas as an extreme microadventure, where it's less about going slow and enjoying the moment and more about pushing yourself to the limits but under your own terms. You're in control of when you stop, what route you take and how quickly you need to complete the challenge. And although there needs to be a sense of achievement – whether it's simply completing the distance or, in cases like Race a Mountain Train, actually winning – you're not meant to take them too seriously. After all, this is supposed to be fun.

Monopoly Marathons

RACE YOUR WAY THROUGH THE MONOPOLY STREETS

PREPARATION TIME
2 HOURS

ADVENTURE TIME
3-7 HOURS

Yes

1 **2** 3 4 5
DIFFICULTY

 CONCEPT

If you love playing Monopoly, then this challenge will be right up your street! With the game licensed in 103 countries and hundreds of cities, you can use your local Monopoly board as a template to create a route that connects all the streets, stations and utility companies into a marathon route to rival the best.

RULES

1. You can start and finish the run wherever you like, but you must visit all the points on your Monopoly board.

2. Take a photo of yourself at each of the place names to prove you've visited them.

KIT

- Running shoes
- Map
- GPS
- Camera

METHOD

As an adult, New Year's Eve can be a tricky time of year. We're often pressured to do something special, go out with friends and party the night away, only to wake up on the first day of the year feeling decidedly the worse for wear. But my childhood memories are very different. After a family dinner, we'd sit around the fire as my parents brought out the Monopoly board for our annual game. Some years, I'd be rubbing my hands together with joy if I managed to buy the posh Mayfair or Park Lane and in other years, I'd be cursing my poor fortune for being landed with the less salubrious Whitechapel or Old Kent Road.

Although Monopoly's origins lie in the United States, it's now licensed in 103 countries, available in thirty-seven languages and for hundreds of cities around the world, including forty-eight in France, thirty-five in Germany and eight in Spain. And if you can't find your local edition, you could always create your own customised version with a printer and a little creative licence.

Reminiscing about my childhood, I asked my long-suffering wife if she'd like to have a game of Monopoly with me on New Year's Eve. She gave me a slightly perplexed look. 'No, no,' I explained. 'This is much better – we're going to run a marathon around the Monopoly board.'

Now, of course, if you were to play by the rules and make this a true test of endurance, you'd be casting dice, going to jail, spending money and running a lot further than a marathon. Or you could run between the streets in whichever order they appear on the board – equally taxing.

But I've saved those ideas for another day. On this occasion, and keen to avoid divorce on New Year's Eve, we printed out a map and plotted

✓

IF YOU LIKE THE SOUND OF THIS, THEN TRY:

nohtaraM ehT

Boundaries Run

60 Minutes

Peak to Peak

Hut to Hut

the twenty-two streets, four railway stations and two utility companies from the Monopoly board. All we then had to do was connect the dots – starting and finishing at our home.

A sensible person would argue that for practicality's sake, it's probably best not to do this at peak rush hour, let alone on the busiest night of the year when many of the roads are closed except to ticket holders. But in some way, our hare-brained scheme added to the challenge. And what better way to see in the New Year than running a marathon around a Monopoly board and hopefully catching the fireworks at the same time? Plus, we'd not wake up with a hangover!

By the time New Year's Eve arrives, we are almost tempted to ditch the trainers and grab our bikes (which is another valid option), but we decide to stick to the original plan on the basis that it will be a lot easier to move around the city on foot than by bike. And we are right.

With twenty-eight places to visit, we find ourselves taking sneaky back streets in an effort to avoid the hordes of revellers, tourists or the occasional roadblock. And to mark our progress, we pose for a photograph beside each of the place names, grinning at the camera with childish delight at our exciting game of endurance meets chance.

There's something exhilarating about following an invisible route – one that only you can see – whether that's from your map or GPS. And when you consider that the place names on a Monopoly board are often what are considered to be 'must visit' locations, this is the ultimate tourist run.

However, our initial exuberance occasionally wanes as tired legs and a lack of carbs gets the better of us. But luckily, this is easily remedied by nipping into the local fish and chip shop for some guilt-free sustenance.

It's understandable that we receive a few funny looks from passers-by, but upon questioning, any surprise quickly turns into comments of 'What a brilliant idea' or 'I'd love to do that' as they realise the attraction of running

a marathon around the most famous streets of their city.

Arriving home at 1 a.m., having run just shy of 50 kilometres in a smidgeon over 6 hours, we collapse on the sofa and open a bottle of champagne to celebrate. As we toast each other's good fortune, we both agree it was the toughest game of Monopoly we've ever played, but by far the most enjoyable.

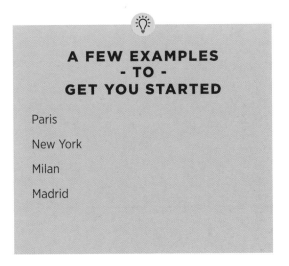

A FEW EXAMPLES
- TO -
GET YOU STARTED

Paris

New York

Milan

Madrid

Wild at Heart

PREPARATION TIME
3 HOURS

ADVENTURE TIME
3-10 HOURS

No

1 2 **3** 4 5
DIFFICULTY

CONCEPT

If you've not yet heard, SwimRun is the new triathlon. A sort of mashup between wild swimming and trail running, the concept is simple – to run and swim between lidos, lakes, rivers and dams.

RULES

1. This is a self-supported challenge.

2. All lakes/pools/sea should be publicly accessible.

3. Any form of swim aid is acceptable, but you must carry what you use from start to finish.

KIT

- Wetsuit
- Goggles
- Trail running shoes (lightweight)
- Swim cap
- Hand paddles (if preferred)
- Waterproof map case

METHOD

It's bizarre to think an idea that started off as a drunken bet – to swim and run across the Stockholm Archipelago – has now become a sport that's one of the most talked about in the world. It's also one of the fastest-growing.

All thanks to two friends, Michael Lemmel and Mats Skott from Sweden, who co-founded the ÖTILLÖ – a 75-kilometre adventure race between twenty-six islands.

When the ÖTILLÖ launched in 2006 (*ötillö*

TOP TIPS?

Use a pull buoy to keep your hips afloat while swimming.

If you're going to use hand paddles, practise with them beforehand.

is Swedish for Island to Island), it was the first event of its kind in the world. Sitting very much on the fringe of endurance sports, it attracted those adventure athletes looking for something new, something fresh and, most importantly, something that sounded bloody difficult. More than ten years later, the ÖTILLÖ has grown in ways its founders could never have predicted, boasting a roster of events all over Europe.

But no one enters a SwimRun event with the idea of setting Personal Bests or chasing an arbitrary time. Rather it's about 'moving through nature', as co-founder Mats Skott once said. And if there was ever a sport where I felt most connected to nature, it's doing a SwimRun.

The hardest part in planning your own SwimRun is simply getting your head around the concept. Although there are a few similarities, SwimRun is very different from a triathlon in that you're totally self-sufficient and carry the same equipment throughout the entire race. Which means you've got to swim in your trainers and run in your wetsuit.

Most people can't imagine running more than a hundred yards in a wetsuit, let alone running an ultra marathon. And then there's the fear of the cold open water. And just to make

life increasingly difficult, you've got the strange sensation of swimming with your shoes on. On paper, it sounds bonkers. But in reality, it's one of the most exhilarating experiences you'll ever have.

Remember, you don't need any specialist kit to do a SwimRun. If you've got an old wetsuit lying around, cut off the legs and arms at the joints – giving you better mobility when you run and lessening the chance of overheating. An old pair of trail shoes will also do – and if you think they're on the heavy side, drill some holes in the soles to help with drainage. The only other bits of kit that come in handy are goggles and a swim cap.

Don't worry if you don't have an archipelago nearby. Instead, why not run between lakes and swim across them? With more than half a million natural lakes with a surface area greater than 10,000m² in Europe, there is plenty of choice. Finland has the lion's share with a mind-boggling 188,000 lakes, more than any other country in the world. However, you need only a couple of lakes to create a route – just make sure you have permission.

And if you live in a city, outdoor swimming pools work almost as well. You could create an urban route linking them up, although you might get the odd glance from passing strangers.

✓
IF YOU LIKE THE SOUND
OF THIS, THEN TRY:

Urban Tri

Tri-It-Yourself

Hidden Waters

Source to Sea

Regardless, it's best not to bite off more than you can chew, so your first SwimRun should be simply getting used to transitioning from water to land and back again using just one lake/pool/reservoir. Working out what kit works and doesn't, how to carry water and food – it all takes a bit of practice. And that's part of the adventure. Because after you've done your first SwimRun, everything else will feel boring.

A FEW EXAMPLES
- TO -
GET YOU STARTED

Isles of Scilly

Finland - the Land of a Thousand Lakes

The Swimmer - London

nohtaraM ehT

RUN THE ROUTE OF AN OFFICIAL RACE IN REVERSE

PREPARATION TIME
1 HOUR

ADVENTURE TIME
2-5 HOURS

No

1 **2** 3 4 5
DIFFICULTY

CONCEPT

If you find yourself without an entry for your local marathon or half, don't despair. With the signed, traffic-free route being empty on race morning, why not run the route in reverse, starting at the finish and finishing at the start.

RULES

1. Make sure you understand the route – on non-race days, it may be busier and need your full attention.

2. Try to start as close to the official finish as possible.

KIT

- Trail running shoes
- Running pack/vest
- Spare warm clothes
- Water
- Food
- GPS watch

METHOD

As Big Ben prepares to strike 4 a.m. on an early Sunday morning in late April, a small group of runners stand beneath it, chatting amiably with each other as they limber up. In just a few short hours and with almost 26 miles behind them, the fastest runners in the world will speed past this very stretch of road on their way to Pall Mall in the hope of calling themselves the winner of the London Marathon.

But this group of runners, some of whom are in fancy dress, are not there to race. They're waiting for any last-minute arrivals to join them on the ghostly quiet streets that wind their way through 26.2 miles of London. They're running in the nohtaraM nodnoL. No, this is not a spelling mistake, but London Marathon in reverse. And with Big Ben being the closest they could get to the finish line of the event itself, they're about to run the route in reverse, finishing in Greenwich where tens of thousands had been nervously waiting to start their own race.

It's not exactly a new concept. In fact, among the ultra running community there are a growing number of gritty individuals, who every year will attempt what's known as a 'double' –

essentially running the reverse route of a race and then turning around to take part in the actual event.

So, if you missed out on a place for your chosen race, especially a big city marathon or one of the world Marathon Majors, why not try them in a different way and on any day, and do nohtaraM ehT? The only thing you'll not get is a bib number and a medal. Other than that, you're still running a marathon – worth bragging rights on its own!

Depending upon where you live, almost every city and town will at some point in the year host a race. It doesn't have to necessarily be a marathon – the same rules apply for a 10k, half marathon or, at the other end of the spectrum, an ultra marathon. Although it's normally the mainstream marathons that have closed traffic-free roads, even small races have the route signposted the day before. After all, just because you don't have a race entry, it doesn't mean that you can't follow the route. Remember, it's closed to cars, not pedestrians.

If you choose to race the night before a race, you'll have to prepare yourself for an early wake-up call, especially if you're running a marathon distance (or more). You need to make sure you are not in anyone's way, and leave plenty of time to finish ahead of the race.

Unlike most marathons, for nohtaraM ehT you'll need to be relatively self-sufficient. The energy stations spaced every mile won't be open for business at 4 a.m. Nor will there be a ready stream of volunteers handing you bottles of water. Nope, you'll have to fend for yourself, bringing with you sufficient water to last anything from three to five hours or more. But this is what makes the nohtaraM ehT so attractive.

If you're looking for a Personal Best, this is probably not the time to try for one. This is a time to spend with friends, enjoy the moment and not think too much. In fact, you should try to do the opposite. In a race like the London Marathon, where the support from the crowds lining the road can actually be an assault on your senses, here you'll find such peace and quiet that it will be eerie.

As the runners approach Greenwich, they almost blend in with the thousands of other runners making their way to the official start. Most of those with bib numbers on will never in a million years think you've just run the route in reverse. But as they nervously wait for their race, unless you're planning on turning around and running the main event, this is your chance to put your feet up and have a cup of tea – as you watch everyone else prepare to run 26.2 miles.

A FEW EXAMPLES
- TO -
GET YOU STARTED

London Marathon – April

Paris Marathon – April

Rome Marathon – March

Berlin Marathon – September

New York Marathon – November

Sea to Summit

RUN OR CYCLE FROM THE SEA TO A PROMINENT HIGHPOINT IN THE REGION

PREPARATION TIME
2 HOURS

ADVENTURE TIME
1-6 HOURS

Yes

1 2 **3** 4 5
DIFFICULTY

 CONCEPT

If you can't decide whether you like the sea or mountains, then this uphill, Sea to Summit challenge will be right up your street. With almost all elevation figures being based on 'above sea level', you'll get an extra sense of satisfaction knowing that you've gone from the lowest point to the highest point. For some, it will be about how quickly you get to the top while for others, it's simply the reward of going from sea to summit.

✎ **RULES**

1. You must be self-supported during the challenge – which means, no outside assistance that isn't readily available to anyone else.

2. It must be done in one continuous push. If you're creating a multiday option, then it should be in consecutive days.

◎ **KIT**

- Map
- GPS
- Compass
- Running shoes
- Small running pack
- Water
- Food

🦶 METHOD

It's strange how it is so easy to take for granted what is on your doorstep. And how easy it is to forget the simple pleasure of poring over a map: tracking contour lines to their highest points, seeing rivers disappear, or working out just how many miles you are from wild settings like national parks. As I trace my finger around the perimeter of my nearest park, the Exmoor National Park, and note that it has a high point of 1,702 feet at Dunkery Beacon, I realise that it is pretty close to the sea. And it is the same for a number of national parks such as Sierra Nevada National Park in southern Spain and Vesuvius National Park in Italy.

Like magic, routes begin to materialise before my eyes: a mixture of footpaths, waymarked trails, off-beat tracks or quiet country lanes, all leading up to a high point and stretching back to the sea. An adventure is created: from Sea to Summit. What an epic way to spend a day!

Although I could have cycled, for this one I pick the old faithful runners – the high point is quite off-piste for the bike, and the potential of hidden trails and sneaking paths beckon the feet to explore them.

The best thing about Sea to Summit is how the planning is relatively quick and easy. Simply decide how far you would like your run to be (it could easily be a good day's trek too), find a suitable high point and then measure back to the sea. Preferring to take the opportunity of finding secret avenues, I pick my two points and allow a compass bearing to do the rest – rather than marking out a specific route.

With map and compass in hand, I set off at a pace and follow any street, path or trail that allows me to keep as close to the crow's line as possible. Of course, if you want to make sure

!

IF THAT'S NOT DIFFICULT ENOUGH:

Why not see if you can go from the lowest point beneath sea level in your country to the highest summit?

you pick the fastest or most accessible route this can be planned on your map beforehand – it's certainly the best way to ensure you take in places of interest, perhaps historic monuments or just a good spot for refreshment. For me, this particular challenge is in the spontaneity and the speed: but on another day …

As I've guessed from reading the contours on the map, the first half of the route is a relatively gentle excursion. It isn't until about 5 miles into the route that I am reminded I have picked myself an uphill challenge – the gradient starting to steepen serving as a reminder that this is, after all, a Sea to Summit challenge and I

TOP TIPS?

You can make this challenge as easy or difficult as you would like, depending upon how far away you choose to make your summit. Of course, if you happen to live in a country that is landlocked or as flat as a pancake, it might seem a challenge, but every country, no matter how flat, has a high point. Who knows, your nearest high point might be the top of a monument – Rocky style.

You need to consider how you're going to get back from the summit. You can make the challenge harder by turning it into a Sea to Summit to Sea. Or you can rope in your family and have them meet you at the top, ready to take you back home!

IF YOU LIKE THE SOUND OF THIS, THEN TRY:

Source to Sea

Race the Sun

Extreme Twinning

still have to climb about 1,700 feet of elevation in the space of 3.5 miles.

The climb is definitely worth it for the big open skies that are my reward for running through a rather thick period of foliage, making sure to check my map along the way to stay on bearing: it would be all too easy to take the wrong path.

Some 15 minutes later I pop out of the woods and am rewarded with a panoramic view of the town and parkland I have already covered. It's a booster to push me up the hardest bit to come – the rounded tip of my summit, and my challenge end.

I use the opportunity to relate where I am to the map, trying to identify recognisable features. Always keeping an eye on my energy levels, of course, in terms of how much further and higher I'm going to climb.

Just when I think the climb is going on forever, I suddenly spot my destination – the trig point that marks the highest point in southern England outside Dartmoor. I use up my last bit of energy in a sprint to the highest point marker and turn around to be rewarded with a beautiful panoramic view of the sea. From here I can etch out the route I've taken to get here and already start planning the next Sea to Summit challenge – a great way to test the legs and earn a 'something new' badge of personal honour.

A FEW EXAMPLES
- TO -
GET YOU STARTED

Hurlstone Point to Dunkery Beacon – Exmoor

Hendaye to La Rhune – Pyrenees

Naples to Mount Vesuvius – Vesuvius National Park

Motril, El Verado, to Mulhacen, the highest mountain in Spain – Sierra Nevada National Park

Neustadt to Bungsberg – the highest point in Schleswig-Holstein, Germany

Race a Mountain Train

TAKE A MOUNTAIN TRAIN UP AND RACE IT DOWN

PREPARATION TIME
2 HOURS

ADVENTURE TIME
2-3 HOURS

 Yes

1 2 3 **4** 5
DIFFICULTY

CONCEPT

Around Europe you'll find a host of stunning mountain train journeys, some short and some longer. Similar to a funicular, some of these mountain trains take you to the summit – ideal for taking your family. But rather than take the train down, you grab your trainers and see if you can race it on foot, while your family waves from the carriages.

 ## RULES

1. The race starts the moment the doors to the train close.

2. You can choose to race the train up or downhill, or even both – whichever one provides the ideal challenge.

KIT

- Trail running shoes
- GPS watch
- Running vest pack (with room for water if necessary)

🦶 METHOD

I try to imagine what they must have been thinking in 1908, when they first came up with the idea of building a railway here, on the French/Spanish border in the heart of the Basque Pyrenees.

If I look east, I can see the vast expanse of the Atlantic Ocean, with a sandy line marking the coastline, stretching away to the north of France. To the south of me, the Spanish Pyrenees fall away towards San Sebastian. And to the west, the snowy peaks of the High Pyrenees beckon, reaching out to me with temptation. But right now, I have other plans.

The guidebook suggests that it takes 2 hours to descend the 4.9-kilometre path to the train station below. And with a drop in elevation of 736 metres, it's not for the faint of heart. If I'm to beat the train, I have just 35 minutes.

'We'll see you at the bottom!' my wife shouts as the train gently starts to move, adding, 'And be careful.' Arms waving, and with their faces pressed against the window, I watch as my family and friends slowly disappear, then I snap out of my dream world. I've almost forgotten that I have a train to race, and my lack of

concentration has given them a tiny head start.

You've probably noticed this, but railway tracks tend to be rather flat. And that's for good reason: trains don't go uphill very well. To overcome this problem, engineers have come up with all sorts of solutions over the ages, from horseshoe curves to zigzags, but the most popular is the rack and pinion railway, first used in 1868 on the still-functioning Mount Washington Cog Railway in the United States.

It's different from a funicular (see page 16), in that rather than using cables and counterweights, the rack and pinion rail tracks have a toothed rail in the centre of the track. This, combined with a cog on the train, allows the train to operate on steep inclines.

Now, it's worth pointing out that unless you have the limbs and speed of the Swiss mountaineer Ueli Steck, it's highly unlikely you'll beat a mountain train going uphill. Having looked at the profile out of the window on my way up La Rhune, I quickly gave up on this idea. However, the descent is a different matter altogether. It's akin to fell running – where you let gravity do all the work.

So Step 1 is fairly obvious, but the crucial ingredient of this challenge is to find a mountain train. Without one, it's simply not going to work. Once again, Wikipedia has a list of rack railways around the world, grouped by country – so you shouldn't have a problem finding one.

The next step is to look at an online map and try to identify your start and finish point,

symbolised by the respective train stations. By far the easiest way to do this is to use Strava, and the help of the Global Heatmap to identify if there are any tracks that will take you down the mountain.

✓
IF YOU LIKE THE SOUND OF THIS, THEN TRY:

Race the Commute

Race to Space

Arch to Arch

Since many of the mountain trains cater for hikers who choose to hike up and take the train down, there's a good chance you'll find a track nearby. It's then simply a case of connecting the dots.

As I follow the yellow arrow-markers down the mountain, I'm having a hard time choosing whether to look at my feet, the spectacular view or the train to my right, where my family are cheering me on from the carriage window. But

with the trail being rockier than I anticipated, I decide I like my teeth where they are, and focus my attention on my footing.

Luckily, the path smooths out and I manage to up my pace, keeping an eye on the time and the train, which is disconcertingly far away. But either it is slowing down, or I am speeding up, and I found myself running alongside the tracks – with the train behind me.

With the train station at the Col de St Ignace growing closer, I feel confident, for the first time in 25 minutes, that I will beat it. And sure enough, 32 minutes after setting off, I arrive – one step ahead of Le Petit Train de la Rhune. I've done it!

A FEW EXAMPLES
- TO -
GET YOU STARTED

Snowdon Train – Snowdonia, Wales

Petit Train de la Rhune – French Pyrenees

The Sassi-Superga Rack Tramway, in Turin, Italy – it takes 18 minutes to run 3 miles downhill. So make it more difficult by trying to run up

The Cog – Mount Washington, USA

Pilatus – Switzerland

Montenvers Mer de Glace – Chamonix, France

Day Flight Run

TAKE A DAY FLIGHT AND COMPLETE AN ADVENTURE CHALLENGE BETWEEN THE FIRST AND LAST FLIGHT OF THE DAY

PREPARATION TIME

4 HOURS

ADVENTURE TIME

24 HOURS

 No

1 2 **3** 4 5

DIFFICULTY

CONCEPT

The essence of this challenge is to see how much you can squeeze in between the first and last flight of the day and, ideally, do it on the cheap. You might cycle around an island, run between a series of peaks, or perhaps even do a mini coast to coast challenge – all before catching the last flight home. Just don't miss it.

RULES

1. The challenge must be completed within a day.

2. There's no limit on how long the flight takes, but ideally it should be as short as possible to maximise on the activity you set yourself.

3. Costs should be kept to a minimum.

KIT

- Running shoes
- Running pack
- GPS watch
- Glasses

METHOD

'Is this your first time to Jersey?' my seat companion asks, unable to contain his curiosity as he watches me inspect the large map of Jersey that I have unfolded on my tray table.

'Yes,' I answer with a certain degree of embarrassment. Despite having flown over the Channel Islands more times that I can count, I've never before looked at them as a destination in their own right. And if it weren't for a casual conversation with a friend from Jersey, I would never have thought about flying to and from the largest of the Channel Islands in day.

If the man next to me is surprised by my first response, he almost spills his coffee when I tell him I am going to meet some friends and then try to run around the island in time for the last flight home.

When I lived in the city, I spent half my time loving it and the rest longing to escape. However, if there's one advantage to living in a concrete jungle, as opposed to the lush but sometimes remote countryside, it's being close to a major airport. And thanks to the plethora of budget airlines popping up all over the place, creating healthy competition for the mainstream carriers,

it's becoming increasingly cheap, especially if you fly without luggage.

The first step in a creating a Day Flight Run is to open up your atlas or Google Maps and have a look at where you could fly to within 90 minutes. You'll often find this information in the back of airline magazines or on the Internet. It was by chance that I noted BA offered a day

TOP TIPS?

There's no reason why you can't take the same principle and apply it to ferries and trains.

If doing a cycling challenge (see Perimeter Bicycling, page 194), consider taking hand luggage only and renting a bike when you arrive.

flight return to Jersey, for a meagre £70. And what's more, it was only a fifty-minute flight.

As the plane begins its descent, I get my first proper glance of my playground for the day, noting with interest how the majestic coastline to the north is in stark contrast to the urban sprawl around its capital to the south. I hope to run the full 48 miles, but after a moment of reflection and speaking with my friends upon arriving at the airport, we decide to jump in a taxi and head to the other side of the island. Consulting our map, we work out the coastline trail is exactly 26 miles long. So depending upon how quickly we get to our notional finish, we could just keep going if time permits.

IF YOU LIKE THE SOUND OF THIS, THEN TRY:

Race the Commute

Race a Mountain Train

There is something magical about an island – whether it's their feeling of remoteness which encourages a degree of self-sufficiency or simply because it makes you feel like you're on holiday. Whatever it is, as I run along the stunning cliffs, passing ancient forts, Second World War bunkers and otherworldly sheep, I feel like I've properly escaped.

In an ordinary marathon, I'd be eating energy gels and bars. But on this occasion, I decide to leave it to chance, instead pausing at any one of the numerous local cafés and pubs for refreshments – so much more nutritious and satisfying to the palate than a sticky energy gel.

However, my propensity to stop and take photos, indulge in the local culinary delights and chat to the locals we pass, means that despite giving myself a generous amount of time, I need

A FEW EXAMPLES
- TO -
GET YOU STARTED

Fly to Bergen, Norway, run the Seven Mountains, fly back

Fly to Vienna and see how much you can complete of the 120km Rundumadum Hiking Trail that encircles the city

to get a move on, or I'll miss my flight.

All of a sudden, having spotted our flight making its approach above us, we find ourselves running like the clappers to the taxi I'd pre-booked at the beach finish point. If ever there is a time to be grateful for having hand luggage only, this is it.

An hour later, as the plane takes off, I look down at the island I've just attempted to run around. And although I didn't complete the entire perimeter, I've had one of the best days of my life.

So the next time you're sitting on a plane, take a casual look at the rear of your airline magazine and see where you can fly to in less than 90 minutes. You'll be surprised by what's on your doorstep, if only you take the time to look.

Castle to Keep

RUN OR CYCLE BETWEEN CASTLES

PREPARATION TIME
3 HOURS

ADVENTURE TIME
2-48 HOURS

 Yes

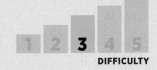
1 2 **3** 4 5
DIFFICULTY

 ## CONCEPT

It's impossible not to get a little bit excited when you see a castle. From the imposing fortress-style schlösser in Germany to the elegant châteaux of France, they remind us of a bygone era, and some date back over a millennium. Taking inspiration from the steeplechase as well as the kings and queens of old, this challenge will see you race between castles and spires, learning a bit about their history along the way.

RULES

1. You should be as self-supported as possible. No outside assistance, but stopping at local shops is fine.

KIT

Running
- GPS
- Running shoes
- Shorts
- Top
- Socks

Cycling
- Bike
- Helmet
- Bike shoes
- Glasses
- GPS

METHOD

When I was a child, I desperately wanted to live in a castle. Of course, back then I had no idea of the upkeep involved, the stress of a leaking roof that requires scaffolding 50 feet high or the fact that in winter you'll long for a decent central heating system and double glazing. No, none of that went through my mind. I was more interested in the history contained within the walls of these fortresses.

In days gone by, the barons, dukes and kings who owned these magnificent strongholds would visit each other's castles, taking journeys lasting from days to months. When I think of the hundreds of miles many would travel, sometimes in the depths of winter, I can't but help be impressed. So this challenge is in part inspired by our aristocratic forebears but also by the modern-day steeplechase, whose origins lie in nineteenth-century Britain, where runners would race each other from church steeple to steeple, jumping over a series of obstacles as they went.

When planning a route of this nature, you want to try and make it as interesting as possible. With only a weekend to squeeze your journey in to, there's no point looking for castles too far

TOP TIPS?

Prior to setting off, plot your route online and download it to your GPS. But make sure you have a backup map. There's nothing worse than running out of batteries.

Take a camera.

IF YOU LIKE THE SOUND OF THIS, THEN TRY:

Arch to Arch

Trail Time Travelling

Extreme Twinning

60 Minutes

apart. In my experience, the best Castle to Keep routes are the ones that recreate an ancient journey or which have an historical connection. It could be two neighbouring castles built to defend against a common enemy (the British or the French, in many cases), and if they're reasonably close together, they might be perfect for fastpacking (see Hut to Hut, page 188) or running between. Or if you fancy becoming the Lord of the Manor for a night, you could make a bicycle journey between any of the 38 castles that have been turned into youth hostels in Germany. All of the perks without the upkeep!

As I was keen to explore my local area and learn new routes, I decided to make a micro bikepacking time trial between some of the principal châteaux scattered around my home in the Pyrénées-Atlantiques. After a short amount of research, I selected five that appealed to me, ranging from the birthplace of Henri IV to a nineteenth-century abandoned fortress built to defend against the Spanish. I plotted the castles on the map and created a circular loop with a few detours, all following the most scenic roads and, where possible, the odd col. By the time I'd made my plan, I was practically shaking with excitement. It felt as though I was off on an historical adventure through time.

What I love about cycling, something that you don't get so much by running, is how you can cover such huge distances in such a short amount of time. I mapped out a journey of 150 kilometres and completed it in a weekend. Here I was, discovering one charming village after another, giving me plenty of excuses to stop and stock up on croissant and pastries in the local boulangeries. In between, I'd pedal along the quiet country lanes, breathing in the fresh air like a sommelier would sniff a glass

A FEW EXAMPLES
- TO -
GET YOU STARTED

Cycle from Lourdes to Foix in the French Pyrenees

Cycle or run from Windsor Castle to Buckingham Palace

Cycle or run from the Royal Palace of Madrid to El Escorial, Spain

of red wine, but my focus was always on the next castle.

Just as steeples were easy for runners to see from long distances, castles are too. The medieval ones are commonly built on hills, not only a perfect place to defend from but a good vantage point. Whereas some of the nineteenth-century châteaux have fabulous towers shooting up into the sky, you only need to head into neighbouring Germany or Austria for true height – the castles here even make Harry Potter's Hogwarts look small.

Having done my research beforehand, I'd stored some of the castles' history on my phone, allowing for an electronic self-guided tour before taking an obligatory photo or two and then moving on to the next. Countless villages, five castles and 150 kilometres later, I was almost sad to be coming to the end of my journey. Not only had I learned an enormous amount about the history of the region, but I'd created a wonderful cycle route in the process, perfect to share with my friends.

Peak to Peak

CREATE A RUNNING ROUTE THAT CONNECTS PROMINENT HIGH POINTS

PREPARATION TIME
4 HOURS

ADVENTURE TIME
3-24 HOURS

No

1 2 3 4 5
DIFFICULTY

💡 CONCEPT

Inspired by the Bob Graham Round, Peak to Peak involves running between the highest points in a region using only a map and compass (or GPS). It's an opportunity to create your own round, whether it lasts 4 hours or 24.

🗹 RULES

1. The start and finish must ideally be at the same place. Try to find a prominent point – a church, town hall, library, or even a café.

🧭 KIT

- Trail running shoes
- Map
- GPS device
- Running backpack
- Food and water
- Waterproof jacket
- Spare warm top
- Emergency blanket
- Whistle

🐾 METHOD

When I first heard about the Bob Graham Round, a legendary challenge that involves running between the forty-two highest peaks in the Lake District, all within 24 hours, I simply knew I had to do it. For me, and hundreds of other runners, the 66 or so miles of fell running with a backbreaking 27,000 feet of climbing was the ultimate 'hard as nails' way to prove to myself that I was a real runner.

However, as I sat upon a rocky outcrop recovering from running through boggy, un-runnable terrain, I realised that I'd bitten off a little more than I could chew. I was some 16 hours and 48 long miles into my first attempt, but I'd

TOP TIPS?

If you're new to mountain running, don't be too ambitious on creating your first Peak to Peak. Try and create a small, 3-4 hour route to begin with before going big.

clearly not spent enough time chasing chickens, à la Rocky Balboa. Inadequate preparation meant I would have to temporarily retire my gauntlet. 'Perhaps I should try a smaller version first,' I thought. A sort of Micro Bob Graham, if you will. And ideally, something not too far away.

In the United Kingdom, where this type of challenge flourishes, there are Peak to Peak challenges galore, from the Paddy Buckley Round in Wales to the national Three Peaks challenge. Indeed, there's no reason why you have to go between forty-two peaks, when three do just as good a job.

For this type of challenge, it works best on foot, but there's nothing stopping you from creating a national challenge that involves cycling in between the peaks, before climbing them. Regardless of what you do, you'll need a map of the local area and a compass. It's only by looking at a map that you can appreciate the terrain and, more to the point, identify the high points.

A good starting point, and a way to stop you going bonkers looking at the endless possibilities, is to contain your challenge within the lists that peak baggers so helpfully create for

us. You might make a route between ten of the 212 peaks that stand 3,000 metres high in the Pyrenees. Or if you want to get pedantic, you could limit your search to those peaks with a prominence of 600 metres in the Alps.

As with so many of the challenges in this book, when trying to make your own Peak to Peak round, one of the key ingredients is a

competitive streak. For some, it's enough of a challenge to make it from one peak to the next. But if what if we set a time limit?

Just as a mountain race would have a cut-off, you can create an arbitrary time in which to complete it: 6 hours, 12 hours, 24 hours or longer. It's simply a way of controlling how much time you spend doing something before it becomes unreasonable. But then again, until you try something, you don't actually know.

Another option, and perhaps my favourite kind, is a mini Peak to Peak. This essentially involves an out and back hill climb that starts and finishes in a town/village. Your start point is a church, town hall or other prominent building. You then find the two closest high points, plot a route that takes you there and challenge people to get to the two summits and back within a set amount of time. Better yet, try and encourage a local café/restaurant or even the tourist office to reward individuals with a token gift – a free

IF YOU LIKE THE SOUND OF THIS, THEN TRY:

Peak Bagging

Col Collecting

Arch to Arch

Run the Bridges

Sea to Summit

coffee, for instance – for those who complete the challenge within the cut-off.

I may not have succeeded in completing the Bob Graham Round on my first attempt, but I still managed to have a fantastic adventure and ticked off almost thirty of the peaks in the process. And it's important to remember that the whole point of an adventure is that the outcome is unknown. Until we try, we never know what's possible.

A FEW EXAMPLES
- TO -
GET YOU STARTED

Run between the volcanoes of the Auvergne in France

Run the Welsh 3000ers within 24 hours

Run the Seven Hills of Rome within an hour

Race the Sun

WHAT CAN YOU FIT IN BEFORE THE SUN SETS?

PREPARATION TIME
3 HOURS

ADVENTURE TIME
8-18 HOURS

Moderate

| 1 | 2 | 3 | **4** | 5 |

DIFFICULTY

💡 CONCEPT

You might not always see it, but every morning, rain or shine, the sun will rise. And unless you live in the Arctic Circle – where at the height of the summer, daylight can last all day – at some point the sun will set. The idea behind this race against nature is very simple: to try and outrun the sun, whether running around a lake, up or around a mountain, or along a national trail.

✏️ RULES

1. The race starts and finishes at the official time the sun rises and sets according to the sunrise equation.

2. The challenge should be a journey, whether that be climbing a mountain or running around a large lake.

3. There should be an element of risk, making use of as much of the daylight hours as possible.

🧭 KIT

Cycling
- Road bike
- GPS device
- Windcheater/gilet
- Helmet
- Bike shoes
- Food and water

Running
- Running shoes
- Running pack/vest
- Food and water
- GPS watch

METHOD

'Do you think we'll make it?' my friend asks, as we nervously wait for the start of our pop-up 'ultra' race against the sun. Although it's beginning to get light due to the magical properties of morning twilight (sometimes referred to as 'astronomical dawn'), the sun hasn't officially poked its head above the horizon yet. That will happen at precisely 6:35, at which point we'll have 11 hours, 43 minutes and 30 seconds to run the 60-mile off-road route I've mapped out from London to Brighton.

I am under no pretence that averaging 5.1 miles an hour for an entire day is going to be easy. Considering it's the end of September and the daylight is rapidly fading, I haven't exactly given us plenty of time. But I've done the maths, and if we stay on track, it should be just about doable.

Indeed, thanks to the sunrise equation – which takes into account longitude and latitude, altitude, and the time zone – it's possible to calculate the exact moment the uppermost ray of the sun will poke its head above and below the astronomical horizon. Even if the weather is lousy and the sun is nowhere to be seen, you can

TOP TIPS?

There are plenty of online calculators that will give you the precise time the sun rises and sets according to your location.

Don't be too ambitious.

If doing a point to point, try to find somewhere with a train to take you back home.

be certain it's there – meaning you can do this challenge any day of the year.

For instance, in Paris on 21 June, the longest day of the year, you'll have 16 hours, 10 minutes and 52 seconds to complete your race against the sun. However, at the other end of the scale, the winter solstice will give you a mere 8 hours, 14 minutes and 48 seconds. On the plus side, you don't have to get up quite so early.

There are three steps to racing the sun. First, choose a challenge. Second, determine how long you think you can do it in. Lastly, pick a

date that gives you exactly the right amount of daylight hours to beat the sun.

With endless possibilities, deciding what to do is the hardest part of Race the Sun,

✓

IF YOU LIKE THE SOUND OF THIS, THEN TRY:

Extreme Twinning

Sea to Summit

Arch to Arch

but there's a good chance you'll either do a circular loop, an out and back route or a point to point. If you have the confidence and experience, you could decide to run up and down a mountain. Or around it, for that matter. Every year, the shoe giant ASICS hosts an event in Chamonix where two teams race each other in a relay around Mont Blanc in the hope of not only being the winners but indeed beating the sun.

The circular option – whether that be running/cycling around a lake, city or even around a mountain like Mont Blanc (though this is best done as a relay) – offers the greatest challenge. You might equally choose to complete a Peak to Peak (see page 114) or take on an epic Tri-it-Yourself triathlon (see page 132). Either way, a circular route gives a huge sense of achievement. Plus, there's little room for shortcuts should the going get tough.

An out and back route – whether that be to a prominent high point, a town, or along a river – is, in my experience, the easiest to plan. There's no need to worry about return transport and you've got lots of flexibility in terms of your start/finish point. Plus, if you have friends and family in support, it makes their life and yours much easier.

The third option, of a point to point, best lends itself to running a national trail, or cycling from one town to another (see Extreme Twinning, page 182) or indeed, as we were doing, running to the coast.

Deciding how long it will take you is a bit of trial and error. A top tip is to use an online mapping tool, like Strava or MapMyRun, which predicts how long it will take you. Or if you know the mileage, you could use a pace calculator based on what you think you can sustain for x number of hours.

The final stage is to simply pick a date that gives you sufficient amount of time to complete the challenge. Which, as it turns out, I manage to do. Eleven hours and forty minutes later, my friend and I stumble onto Brighton Pier feeling like intrepid warriors returning from battle. With three minutes to spare, we've done it. We've beaten the sun. All we have to do now, is have a well-earned drink and get home. 'Anyone know where the train station is?'

A FEW EXAMPLES
- TO -
GET YOU STARTED

Summer Solstice – run the 78-mile Capital Ring around London

Run in a relay around Mont Blanc

London to Brighton

YoYo Peaks

RUN/CYCLE UP/DOWN ALL OF THE POSSIBLE ROUTES OF A PEAK/COL IN ONE PUSH

 **PREPARATION TIME**
4 HOURS

 **ADVENTURE TIME**
6-36 HOURS

 **Moderate**

 **4** DIFFICULTY

 ### CONCEPT

Whether we're an alpine mountaineer, a cyclist, a climber or a trail runner, one thing is certain: we love going uphill. Climbers look for new routes and pitches. Trail runners sprint up vertical kilometres, mountaineers want to conquer summits, and cyclists get a kick out of riding up the toughest cols or mountains they can find.

Drawing inspiration from the Club des Cinglés du Mont-Ventoux, the concept of YoYo Peaks is to ascend a prominent high point by three or more methods or routes.

RULES

1. There must be at least three or more ways to ascend the mountain, col or hill.

2. To make it accessible to everyone, it should be on public land.

3. It should be made in one attempt.

KIT (if cycling)

- Road bike
- GPS computer
- Windcheater/gilet
- Helmet
- Bike shoes
- Food and water

METHOD

Nestled in the heart of the Provence region of southern France is an ominous-looking mountain that goes by various names. Some call it the Beast of Provence, others the Bald Mountain. Regardless of its nickname, Mont Ventoux, sitting at an elevation of 1,912 metres, is a thing of twisted beauty. It might be of little interest to a mountaineer, but to a cyclist it is Everest. And it's on this legendary and topographical marvel of a mountain, featured in many a Tour de France, that hundreds of cyclists every year will attempt to qualify for membership of one of cycling's most prestigious clubs: the Cinglés du Mont-Ventoux.

In order to become a member of this club (*cinglés* in French loosely translates as 'crazies'), you need to ascend Ventoux from each of the three main roads to the summit, stamping your brevet-styled card as you go. Ironically, of the sixty nationalities who've successfully completed the challenge, the largest contingent come from one of the flattest countries in Europe – the Netherlands.

And it's not just on Mont Ventoux that you can find this type of athletic endeavour. You could head to the Alps and attempt to become a Grand Master of the Fêlés du Grand Columbier or tackle Les Barons du Soulor in the French Pyrenees. But with thousands of cols and mountains to choose from, there's nothing stopping you from creating your own version of this challenge.

Since the crucial element that binds YoYo Peaks together is the possibility of reaching the top by three or more means, your first step is to grab a 1:25,000 map and scour your local area for a suitable candidate. It doesn't necessarily have to be a mountain – simply a prominent

TOP TIPS?

Upon finding a suitable hill/col/mountain, it's wise to recce each of the climbs individually before you attempt to do them all in one day.

If road cycling, think about your gearing and consider whether you need a compact chainset.

high point. It's likely that some options will be better suited to running and others to cycling. It may even be that you do a combination of both, with a mountain biking option chucked in for good measure.

However, more often than not the best types of climbs are the iconic ones. Some, like La Pierre du Saint Martin in the Pays Basque, have seven routes up to the col, which lends itself to seeing how many you can complete in 24 hours. Or you simply select a minimum of three and see how it goes. Whichever option you go for,

IF YOU LIKE THE SOUND OF THIS, THEN TRY:

Race the Funicular

Peak Bagging

Col Collecting

Everesting

A FEW EXAMPLES
- TO -
GET YOU STARTED

Fêlés du Grand Colombier, France

Club des Cinglés de Mont Ventoux, France

Seven Ascents of La Pierre de Saint Martin, France

Les Barons du Soulor – three ascents up the Col du Soulor from Laruns, Argelès-Gazost and Arthez d'Asson, France

Brevetto del Grappa (Italy) – climb the ten ascents up Mont Grappa

the idea is that it's done in one push rather than spread out over a number of days. (For that type of challenge, see 7 in 7, page 206).

There also needs to be a definable start point for each route – a village, trailhead or prominent marker – something that indicates the beginning of the climb. But it could equally be a café, restaurant or even a supermarket, all good places to stock up on morale-boosting refreshments.

Like every Race-it-Yourself adventure in this book, a challenge of this nature is best completed with mates. Although there's nothing wrong with doing it alone, and hats off if you do, a shared goal is so much more fun. All you need to do is pick a hill or col, set a date, gather some friends together to train with and then do it. Rest assured, it will bring a whole new dimension to what you consider 'difficult'.

Tri-It-Yourself

CREATE YOUR OWN TRIATHLON

PREPARATION TIME
5 HOURS

ADVENTURE TIME
2-15 HOURS

Moderate

1 2 **3** 4 5
DIFFICULTY

 CONCEPT

If that Ironman or triathlon event that you wanted to do is booked up, don't despair. Simply create your own bespoke race incorporating your favourite places to swim, ride and run.

 RULES

1. There should be at least three stages, although it can follow a duathlon format if the terrain suits it and there's a lack of somewhere to swim.

2. The course should be publicly available and not be on private terrain.

3. If seasonal, information should be shared on when it's possible to take on the event for others to follow.

KIT

- Bike
- Bike shoes
- Helmet
- Gilet
- Bottle
- Wetsuit
- Goggles
- Running shoes
- Food
- GPS

👣 METHOD

How often have you come across a genius, madcap race that involves traversing mountain ranges, jumping out of a car ferry and swimming across a freezing cold fjord or mountain biking across a desert and thought: How in the hell did they come up with that idea? Well, more often than not, it involved a few drinks and some idle chitchat around a bar.

Today, Ironman World Championships involve a rough 2.4-mile sea-swim, followed by a 112-mile windy bike leg (reduced from 115 miles) and then a marathon in the baking heat. When the concept was first discussed over some drinks at an awards ceremony in Hawaii back in 1977, it began as a dare. Unable to decide which was the toughest, they decided that the only

way to see if it was possible to tackle the three iconic challenges on the island in one day was simply to give it a go. And so a date was set for 7 a.m., 18 February 1978. Only fifteen people took part in the inaugural self-supported test event. Almost forty years later, it's one of the biggest events in the world and consequently sells out like hot cakes. But if you missed out on a slot or couldn't afford the entry fee, there's nothing stopping you creating your own triathlon.

Indeed, for you to do justice to this Tri-It-Yourself challenge, you've got to think outside of the box. With a map in hand, you need to look at the lay of the land and, with military cunning, see how you can combine geographical features with multi-sport challenges. Because if the Urban Tri (see page 40) is designed to be something you can fit into your working week, this challenge is definitely reserved for the weekend. And ideally, is one that requires training. Otherwise, any Tom, Dick and Harry could do it.

The first rule to this challenge is that anything goes. Think big. If necessary, apply a liberal sprinkling of alcohol to aid clarity of thought. By definition, a triathlon involves a swim, cycle and run, but there's nothing to stop you from changing those activities to what suits either your skill set, or the environment. Or even adding a fourth leg and making it a quadrathlon.

Or maybe you can make a mashup of an XTerra triathlon (swim, mountain bike, trail run) with the ÖTILLÖ (a SwimRun between lakes or islands, see page 79). It's subversive races like these and others – including the Norseman Xtreme Triathlon in Norway, an iron distance triathlon considered to be the toughest in the world, and the Inferno Triathlon in Switzerland, a punishing swim, road bike, mountain bike and trail run – that have inspired me to send off my application form. Most importantly, they're less of a race and more of an adventure, where simply finishing is more important than how fast you do it.

You'll have two choices – a linear A to B route, or a circular one that brings you back to your start point. In a linear route, clearly you'll need to think about transition areas and therefore where you're going to drop off your bike and pick up running kit. Both have their advantages, except that the former will certainly require some form of support crew and also allows for greater creativity. Could you cross a mountain range? Or perhaps, you could create a route that connects several islands? Almost anything is possible depending upon whether you're supported or self-supported.

Having decided on a geographical area – whether that be near your home or further afield – the first step is to find somewhere to swim. For instance, do you have a lake, reservoir or perhaps the sea nearby? Perhaps there's a body of water well known to open-water swimmers and one with bragging rights attached to it. Bingo – that's the first stage sorted! Ideally, you want to transition from the swim to the bike, so that your cycle route starts where your swim ends.

It doesn't need to be an Ironman distance. Instead, see if there is an epic, downhill mountain-bike route near you. Is it possible to ride up the hill via a double track and then, similar to an Enduro event, speed down the single track? Or maybe there are some super-tough cols that on their own would be enough of a challenge but, when sandwiched in between a

swim and run, would be epic? It needs to sound bonkers for you to get excited and equally rope your friends in too.

All you now need to do then is find somewhere to run – certainly my favourite element of a triathlon and, equally, where you can have the most amount of fun. Rather than do the usual three to four laps on a road, why not instead go for a trail run around a peak or, for those with grit, up the peak and back?

If you're going 'self-supported', you need to think about whether you can carry enough food and water for your needs. You could use a small running pack to carry supplies. Of course, this totally depends upon how far you plan to go and whether you managed to persuade your friends and family to get involved.

The final stage is to set a date. There's no point in coming up with this epic plan and then letting it go by the wayside. If you tell people what you're doing, you'll feel more committed to it. And don't forget, it's so much more fun doing these events with others. There's no better way to bond than training for and doing an adventure together.

Everesting

CLIMB THE SAME HILL REPEATEDLY UNTIL YOU REACH THE HEIGHT OF EVEREST

PREPARATION TIME
6 HOURS

ADVENTURE TIME
12-24 HOURS

Moderate

1 2 3 4 **5**
DIFFICULTY

💡 CONCEPT

This is a challenge that is as much about exploring your physiological boundaries as it is about doing something epic. Everesting involves riding up a hill repeatedly until you have reached the accumulative ascent of Mt Everest – all in one continuous ride.

☑ RULES

1. Rides can be of any length, on any hill, on any mountain, but it must be ridden in one attempt, on the same hill and on the same route.

2. You need to reach at least 8,848 metres.

3. Only full ascents count – i.e. you must ride the full length of the climb, not half of it.

🧭 KIT

- Bike
- Helmet
- Lights
- GPS
- Food and water

⬛ METHOD

'This is absolutely nuts!' I say to myself, feeling almost giddy with fatigue as I unclip from my pedals. For the past hour and a half, I've been clinging to my handlebars as I've repeatedly cycled up and down the hill beside my home. Some of my neighbours, who've passed me several times, clearly think I've lost the plot. And despite the fact I've done twenty repetitions up and down this short but wretched hill, which averages a 13 per cent gradient, I've clocked up only 1,000 metres of elevation – not even halfway through what's regarded as a warm-up! This Everesting malarky is clearly as tough as it claims to be.

The idea of climbing Mount Everest, the highest point on the planet, is a notion that has gripped the imagination of many an athlete, adventurer and armchair explorer. However, it's widely accepted that unless you have deep pockets or wealthy sponsors, summiting the 8,848-metre peak will simply remain a pipe dream.

So one day in 2014, a group of hill riders in Australia, who go by the name of Hells 500, flipped the concept on its head. They decided

TOP TIPS?

Make sure you recce your route first.

If road cycling, think about your gearing and consider whether you need a compact chainset.

to virtually cycle up Everest, repeatedly climbing the same hill until they'd reached the accumulated height of the highest peak in the world – all in one ride.

They weren't the first to do this crazy challenge, either. That accolade goes to George Mallory, the grandson of the British explorer by the same name who tragically lost his life on Everest in 1924, several hundred metres short of the summit. Seventy years on and while looking for a way to prepare for his own upcoming expedition on Everest, he was told that Australia's Mount Donna Buang was 'a good place to train'. And so began the seeds of what is now one of cycling's most talked-about challenges.

So where do you start? The beauty of this challenge is that you can Everest just about any hill you want. If you're a sucker for punishment, you could choose the biggest, baddest, hors catégorie climb you can find. Or if you want something a little more gentle and you're happy to grind it out, find a long but gradual ascent – and be prepared for a long day in the saddle. At the other end of the scale, if you're time poor and like pushing the pain barrier, you could choose a short but very steep hill, like the one I slogged my way up outside my home. Regardless of the climb, if you want to be an Everest pioneer, the most important thing is you are the first.

'Riders are limited only by their imagination,' writes Andy Van Bergen, the founder of Hells 500 and everesting.cc, in his blog, 'but it will always be a race to be first. Pick a climb. Try to be first. Everest that. Digitally chisel your name into that sucker forever.'

The first step is to visit everesting.cc and find out if your chosen climb has been Everested. If it hasn't, then you're in luck. If you've managed to find a particularly iconic local climb that hasn't been claimed, then you might want to keep your cards close to your chest, lest someone else beats you to it.

As you can appreciate, logistics have a fairly huge hand in your decision process. If you live near a prominent hill, you're perfectly positioned to rope in your family and friends to be your support crew. Or you can simply bundle everything you need into the back of your car and drive to the bottom of your chosen nemesis, and start from there. But don't forget to familiarise yourself with the rules – of which there are plenty.

Now, if you're thinking, 'This sounds nails, I want to do it,' then you should be aware of the three stages of fun. The first 4,000 metres are a bit of a warm-up. The middle 5,000–7,000 metres are where you start to question your sanity and wonder what on earth you've let yourself in for. And then you hit what's affectionately called in

IF YOU LIKE THE SOUND OF THIS, THEN TRY:

Col Collecting

Race to Space

Bikepacking

Perimeter Bicycling

A FEW EXAMPLES
- TO -
GET YOU STARTED

Tourmalet – 8 laps

Alpe d'Huez – 6 laps

Passo Stelvio – 4 laps

Box Hill – 77 laps

mountaineering terms the 'death zone'. This is the point at which your legs will be screaming at you to stop, to quit this madness. You're probably also falling asleep. And, in between, your brain will be doing backflips as you try to calculate how much further you have to go. Be warned, Everesting is not easy.

And although there's no way to make Everesting easier, you can always make it more difficult. For instance, you could Everest on a single or fixed speed, or take it up a notch and do it off-road on a mountain bike. You could try to set a record for the highest number of repetitions (at the time of writing, 836 by Jeff Morris) or the shortest accumulated distance in a single ride (currently 87 kilometres). The world is your oyster.

This is one challenge you can't simply turn up for – you do need to train. But once you're ready, set a date and get out there and 'digitally chisel' your name into the Hall of Fame. Then no one will be able to take that away from you.

#GoRaceItYourself

LONG-TERM BURNERS

RACE-IT-YOURSELF

Realistically, many of us have time only for challenges we can fit in and around our working week or indeed on the weekend. But occasionally, maybe once or twice a year, we get that urge to do something epic. A challenge that might take a couple of weeks to achieve or, in some cases, a lifetime. It's this kind of adventure, the Long-Term Burners, that you'll find in the following pages.

One of my favourite holidays with my wife was not lying on the beach of a Caribbean island. Rather, it was a five-day adventure running around Mont Blanc. Not only was it our first holiday together, but it was also the first time we'd done anything like this outside the confines of a race.

These challenges are the inspiration for you to take the big step to doing something truly epic. To give yourself a goal that you can plan and discuss, one that might even get you dreaming. So whether you're looking to set a perimeter bicycling world record, create a time trial route between your local town's international twin, or cycle from source to sea, you'll find enough ideas here to keep you going for a lifetime of adventure.

Trail Time Travelling

FOLLOW THE FOOTSTEPS OF OUR FOREBEARS BY FASTPACKING AN HISTORIC TRAIL

 PREPARATION TIME
12 HOURS

 ADVENTURE TIME
12 HOURS– 7 DAYS

 Moderate

1 2 **3** 4 5
DIFFICULTY

CONCEPT

Throughout Europe and beyond are a network of trails that have stood the test of time. Over the course of many years – thousands in some cases – knights, soldiers, monks and authors have put their stamp on these ancient routes. Trail Time Travelling is about grabbing your trail shoes or even your mountain bike, and following in the footsteps of our ancestors, retracing the routes that have shaped our country. Who knows, perhaps you'll set a Fastest Known Time?

🖊 RULES

1. If you're planning on setting a Fastest Known Time, you'll need to ensure you declare your intention and be able to provide proof of your time, using GPS tracking, etc.

🧭 KIT

- Trail running shoes
- Map
- GPS device
- Running backpack
- Food and water
- Waterproof jacket
- Spare warm top
- Emergency blanket
- Whistle

🦶 METHOD

Standing on the brow of a hill, I look down at the enormous neolithic stone circle beneath me, the shadows cast by the stones making them look twice as big. It's a beautiful site and one that I've been visualising over the past three days while running. Yet here I am, only a few steps away from completing my 87-mile journey along Britain's oldest road. On the one hand I'm relieved to be finishing, but on the other I'm sad that it's almost over.

I'd heard about the magical properties of this particular national trail, which has been trodden by soldiers, monks, pilgrims and farmers over the past five thousand years. But until I'd experienced it for myself, it simply sounded too good to be true. What I did not expect was the immense feeling of peace and tranquility which this, and so many other historic trails, give you.

Most people take six days to walk the waymarked trail, but I choose to run it in three. As I make my way along a chalky ridgeline, I feel as if I'm on a travel escalator through time. I pass neolithic burial chambers, the hill where St George is said to have fought the Dragon, and a prehistoric giant chalk etching of a white horse carved on to the side of a hill. And when I consider how many hundreds of thousands of people have walked, run or cycled along this very path over five millennia, I feel humbled.

The Ridgeway is just one of a number of ancient footpaths scattered across Europe, many of which have now become national trails. Some follow in the footsteps of authors. Others, like the Chemin de la Liberté in the Pyrenees, will retrace escape routes across mountain ranges used during the Second World War. What they all offer beyond your regular hiking trail is an historic sense of purpose. And if it's good enough for hikers and walkers, it's more than ideal for runners.

Whatever trail you decide to follow will be a personal choice. You may be looking for time out from the hustle and bustle of life. But if you're looking for a challenge, maybe to set a Fastest Known Time, then this is it.

Perhaps the most famous of European pilgrim trails is El Camino de Santiago, or the Way of St James. Every year, more than a hundred thousand people make their way to the resting place of St Jacques de Compostelle

IF YOU LIKE THE SOUND OF THIS, THEN TRY:

Hut to Hut

Castle to Keep

Five to Nine

in Santiago, collecting stamps in their pilgrim passport as they go. The majority begin 800 kilometres out at the traditional start of the French Way at St-Jean-Pied-de-Port, but there are over a dozen other routes to choose from, coming from almost every direction in Europe.

The hardest part with any self-supported multiday run is getting accustomed to spending so much time on your feet. At the beginning, your body will not thank you and the first three or four days will be tough. But then on the fifth day, you reach an ethereal state of enlightenment. You'll wake up not feeling stiff, not that you've run 100 kilometres. Running with a pack will just feel normal.

The key is to take the bare minimum. And since most of the historic trails – in particular the pilgrim routes – offer a plethora of accommodation options often at budget prices, you should be able to keep your pack light enough to make it possible to cover even greater distances.

There is, of course, nothing stopping you from cycling many of these paths. For instance, you can just as easily hop on a bike and ride the Camino as well as run it. Or if you're short of time and want an historical titbit, you could ride the 10.6 kilometres from Bellagio on Italy's Lake Como to the chapel of Madonna del Ghisallo, the patron saint of cycling. It might not sound like much of a challenge, but with 500 metres of ascent, you'll be glad it's not any harder.

Making my way down from the hill towards the stone circle, I don't feel sad any more. I am excited, because I know that this is just the beginning of a series of Trail Time Travelling adventures.

A FEW EXAMPLES
- TO -
GET YOU STARTED

El Camino de Santiago – Europe

Cathar Way GR367 – France

Via Francigena – Italy

St Jacob's Way – Austria

Le Chemin de la Liberté – across the Pyrenees

The Clockmakers' Trail – a seventeenth-century trail around the Black Forest

Robert Louis Stevenson Trail – France

Col Collecting

PREPARATION TIME
1 HOUR

ADVENTURE TIME
2 WEEKS– 1 YEAR

No

1 2 3 **4** 5
DIFFICULTY

💡 CONCEPT

This challenge is about bagging cols, something that requires grit, stamina and endurance. And thanks in part to professional bike races like the Tour de France, they have become what summits are to mountaineers. Not only do we get the satisfaction of grinding our way to the top of the col, which often comes with a magnificent view, we then get to hurtle down the other side, all of which is like meth to cyclists and very addictive.

📝 RULES

1. To be eligible to join the Club des Cent Cols, you must have completed at least 100 cols.

2. The minimum threshold for becoming a Member of the Ordre des Cols Durs, is 50,000 metres on recognised cols. The highest level attainable is Grand Venerable, on reaching 3,000,000 metres.

🧭 KIT

- Road bike
- GPS computer
- Windcheater/gilet
- Helmet
- Bike shoes
- Food and water

METHOD

I wipe my face again for the umpteenth time, thinking to myself that it shouldn't be possible to sweat this much. But then again, this is the Col d'Aubisque – one of the mythic Tour de France climbs that is part of the affectionately named Circle of Death. As far as cols go, this one is a biggie. And although not especially steep, it's long enough to give my legs a decent run for their money.

I still find it intriguing that as cyclists, we love climbing hills, especially cols. A layman would argue that there's nothing pleasant about riding uphill – after all, it's seriously hard work. But as cyclists, we love to push ourselves and, let's face it, unless you're doing a time trial, the flat stuff ain't as fun as the lumpy bits.

To many a cyclist, col collecting is serious business. Thanks in part to the Tour de France, La Vuelta, Il Giro and various other professional bike races, we watch our cycling heroes grind their way up these vertical monstrosities, faces etched in pain, inspiring us to follow in their pedal strokes.

Since moving to the French Pyrenees, I've found myself surrounded by cols – from small

ones that take 15 minutes to climb, to iconic legends like the Aubisque and the Tourmalet, which can take more than an hour. Just as a mountaineer will seek to reach the summit of an 8,000-metre peak, so does a cyclist want to tick off a col. And with a bit of planning, you can accumulate a bucket list of cols that will open doors to a whole new world. And you need only look to the French for inspiration.

In France, climbing cols is practically a national pastime. So much so, there are various clubs you can aspire to join regardless of nationality. One of the most famous mountain cycling clubs in the world, and the largest, is the Club des Cent Cols (CCC). Founded in 1972 in the mountain town of Annecy, it's been a veritable purveyor of cols for the past four decades. But if you want to be a part of this brotherhood, you've got to earn your place – by climbing at least 100 different mountain passes, with at least five of them being higher than 2,000 metres.

It sounds a lot, but for its members who come from all over the world, this is just a starting point. There are, at last count, more than 10,000 cols in France alone, almost 3,400 in Italy, 877 in Germany and an unfathomable 16,211 in Spain. And those are just the ones logged by the Club des Cents Cols. You'll probably find you already have a number ticked off. But if you need a bit of a head start or want to save time planning, then

you could do one of their permanent routes, in France, Italy, Spain or one of the other countries around Europe. These are cycle rides that can be done in one continuous push or broken up into stages, but which will see you climbing the required 100 cols eligible for membership.

Another option is L'Ordre des Cols Durs. Founded in 1960 and run by the Union des Cyclotouristes Toulousains, it's one of the oldest clubs in France. Its aim is to encourage cyclists to ride in the mountains, but for those long-

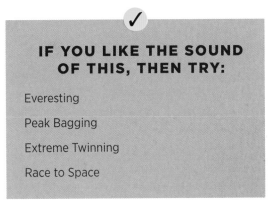

✓

IF YOU LIKE THE SOUND OF THIS, THEN TRY:

Everesting

Peak Bagging

Extreme Twinning

Race to Space

distance cyclists and cycloclimbers who were already converted, it gave them a whole new purpose. More than fifty years later, it has close to a thousand members.

Having achieved the basic membership criteria of 50,000 metres, there are eight official grades to aspire to, starting as an Officer for those who've accumulated 100,000 metres of claims, to the distinguished sounding Grand Venerable once you reach 3,000,000 metres. Although it sounds daunting, it's not quite as difficult as it sounds, since the 'claimable' figure is for the col's, or mountaintop's, official height above sea level, rather than metres climbed. The only caveat is that you must be on a bike or other two-wheeled human-powered contraption, whether it be a recumbent bicycle or tricycle.

So yes, after many years of climbing cols, I can say it's still, simply, a lot of hard work. The reward? Well you've got to find that extra bit out for yourself. But one thing I can tell you, it will bring a whole new dimension to your cycling.

A FEW EXAMPLES
- TO -
GET YOU STARTED

Ride the Cent Cols permanent brevet around the Alps – 100 cols bagged

The Pyrenean Raid, a coast-to-coast journey of 800 kilometres, ticking off 18 cols

Source to Sea

JOURNEY FROM THE SOURCE OF A RIVER TO THE SEA

PREPARATION TIME
2 DAYS

ADVENTURE TIME
2-28 DAYS

Moderate

4
DIFFICULTY

💡 CONCEPT

For those cultures, societies and communities that rely on them, rivers have been their lifeblood for thousands of years. Not only are they a source of water for domestic, industrial and agricultural usage, but they also provide access to trade as well a source of power generation. The Nile, the Tiber, the Euphrates, the Tigris – all are of immense economic and historical value. But only by going to the source can you fully appreciate the flow of a river.

🖊 RULES

1. The journey must start at its source, whether that be a spring, stream, lake or bog, even if it means starting on foot before moving to a bike.

2. The finish is marked by a prominent marker close to the sea.

🧭 KIT

- Bike
- Helmet
- Bikepacking kit
- Bike shoes
- Food and water
- Gilet

METHOD

Creating a journey from source to sea isn't a new idea. Ed Stafford, a former British Army captain, and his Peruvian companion, Cho, completed one of the greatest Source to Sea adventures of history, a feat many thought impossible: to reach the mouth of the Amazon. It took them 859 days and 4,000 miles. Another Brit, Levison Wood, was the first to walk the length of the Nile – the world's longest river – from its source at Lake Victoria. And then there's Australian Mark Kalch, who's currently attempting to paddle the longest river on each of the seven continents.

These are all incredible expeditions, worthy of their place in the history books. However, most of us don't have the time or the resources to make such journeys. But don't fear, it's possible for us mere mortals to complete a Source to Sea, without necessarily costing very much.

There are well over a thousand rivers in Europe, with 150 of those crossing the borders of two or more countries. But where to start? To appreciate a challenge of this magnitude, you first need a map. Then you decide where you want to go and how much time you have to spare.

To find the source, you need to look to the hills and the mountains, where almost all rivers start life as a tiny stream or rill – the result of rainwater or melting snow and ice. From there, rills become gullies, tributaries are formed as other streams join, and then a river is formed, eventually making its way to the sea. However, the source of some rivers will be from where a natural spring releases water from underground, such as the River Thames or the Seine. And

other rivers are formed from lakes, as is the case with the Nile or the Rhine.

Trying to determine what rivers are navigable by foot or bicycle takes a little bit of research – which is part of the fun. But it's often easier to trace a river backwards from its mouth rather than trying to find a trickle of water high up in the mountains. However, a quick search on Google will quickly point you in the direction of its source.

Of course, the best way to navigate a river from its source to sea is by canoe or kayak. But if

A FEW EXAMPLES
- TO -
GET YOU STARTED

GR3 – 1,250 kilometres along the Loire, from its source at Mont Gerbier-de-Jonc to its mouth at La Baule

Rhine Cycle Route, 1,233 kilometres – EuroVelo 15 (Switzerland, Germany, France, Netherlands)

Rhone River – EV17 – Switzerland and France

EV6 – Rhine to Atlantic

Run the 338 miles of the Mosel from its source in the Vosges mountains in France

Elbe Cycle Route – Germany's second longest river

Run the Thames incorporating the waymarked Thames Towpath National Trail to its mouth in the North Sea

✓
IF YOU LIKE THE SOUND
OF THIS, THEN TRY:

Sea to Summit

Run the Bridges

Hidden Waters

Wild at Heart

this is beyond your skill set, and given that many rivers stretch for hundreds of kilometres, you are likely to choose to cycle this particular challenge.

Perhaps one of the most famous, and certainly the highest on my bucket list of Source to Sea routes by bike, is the Rhine Cycle Route. Starting at the beautiful Lake Toma, some 2,345 metres high up in the Swiss Alps, you'll follow a 1,233-kilometre waymarked route along one of Europe's longest rivers. It's a journey that will take you through four countries and nine UNESCO World Heritage sites until you reach its journey's end – the North Sea. Passing the magnificent Rhine Falls; the gorges of the Anterior Rhine, known as the Ruinaulta (or the Swiss Grand Canyon); as well as schlösser galore, it really is a fabulous adventure waiting to happen.

There's no reason why you have to do it all in one go. Many of these routes can be broken up into stages, especially those that lend themselves to being done on foot. Where there's a river, there will be a town – making it possible to rejoin a section by public transport, before continuing your journey. Regardless of how you do it, this will be one of the greatest adventures you'll have.

Arch to Arch

RACE YOUR WAY BETWEEN THE FAMOUS TRIUMPHAL ARCHES

 PREPARATION TIME
6 HOURS

 ADVENTURE TIME
48 HOURS– 7 DAYS

 No

 1 2 3 **4** 5
DIFFICULTY

CONCEPT

The Arc de Triomphe in Paris is one of the most famous monuments in the world. But it's only one example of a triumphal arch, with dozens more scattered throughout Europe and other parts of the world.

📝 RULES

1. This is a time trial between two arches, but they should be of the same era or type, e.g. Roman, post-Roman or natural.

🧭 KIT

- Bike
- Helmet
- Bikepacking kit
- Bike shoes
- Food and water
- Gilet
- Running kit/mountain bike for the natural arches

METHOD

When I first got into endurance racing, I became fixated upon an event widely regarded as one of the most gruelling challenges in the world: the Enduroman Arch to Arc. Every year, a number of hardy endurance athletes will congregate under London's Marble Arch and from there they will start running towards Dover, some 80 -odd miles away. They'll then attempt to swim the English Channel, in itself a monumental task, before cycling several hundred miles to Paris – their goal being the Arc de Triomphe.

Alas, I've still not yet done the race. But when I discovered that there was another Arc de Triomphe in Marseille, the little grey cells in my

✓ IF YOU LIKE THE SOUND OF THIS, THEN TRY:

Extreme Twinning

Peak to Peak

Sea to Summit

brain got rather animated. What about cycling the Arch to Arc to Arc?

Although this is perhaps an extreme example, it's the inspiration for this challenge, one that encourages you to scour a world map and create a route that connects two or more arches. How you get there and how difficult you want to make your life is, of course, up to you.

The Romans are thought to have invented the triumphal arch, to commemorate important occasions from the death of an emperor to a general's victory. You'll find them scattered around Europe's cities, with the largest concentration obviously in Italy and a decent number in France. However, even after the Fall of Rome, they remained a source of fascination, especially to the likes of Napoleon Bonaparte and the kings of the House of Bourbon.

Incidentally, there is also a third type of arch, one not made by man but naturally carved from the rock. This begs for a different type of journey, one that might be done by mountain bike or by foot, as many of these arches will be found off the beaten path.

Once you've selected your two arches, it's then a case of creating a route between the two. By using online mapping tools such as ViewRanger, RidewithGPS or Strava, you'll be able to map out a route and gain a good idea of how long it will take you.

This type of challenge lends itself perfectly to a bikepacking adventure. That feeling of self-sufficiency as you race between the arches will keep you going, but it will also allow you much greater flexibility about where you stay or the detours you might make.

As is the case with any point-to-point challenge, an important consideration is how you're going to get back. There is always the option of cycling back – an Arch to Arch to Arch …

**A FEW EXAMPLES
- TO -
GET YOU STARTED**

London to Paris to Marseille – 1,290 kilometres

Arc de Triomphe in Paris to the Arch of Constantine, Rome – 1,400 kilometres

Rua Augusta Arch, Lisbon, Portugal to Arc de Triomf, Barcelona, Spain – 1,266 kilometres

Bordeaux to Montpellier via the Canal du Midi, 515 kilometres

Soliders' and Sailors' Arch, Brooklyn, New York City, to Atlantic and Pacific Arches, Washington DC – 480 kilometres

Bikepacking

A FAST AND LIGHT CYCLE JOURNEY

 **PREPARATION TIME** **3 HOURS**

 ADVENTURE TIME **24 HOURS–7 DAYS**

No

 1 2 3 **4** 5 **DIFFICULTY**

 ### CONCEPT

Drawing inspiration from the epic races such as the Tour Divide and the Trans Continental, bikepacking is making a stir in endurance circles. Dismissing the need to carry lots of kit, bikepacking is about going fast and light, staying off the beaten track and discovering new places. You don't need lots of fancy equipment, just a willingness to explore and go without creature comforts for a few days.

RULES

1. The idea is to be self-supported, which means that where you stay or what you eat should be available to anyone repeating the journey.

2. There is no time limit except what you give yourself.

KIT

- Bike
- Helmet
- Bikepacking kit
- Bike shoes
- Food and water bottle
- Gilet

🦶 METHOD

'There, I've done it,' I say to myself as I purposefully click the PAY NOW button on the Eurostar website, consequently booking two one-way tickets from Brussels to London. I lean back in my chair feeling very pleased with myself. All I need to do now is break the news to my wife that we're bikepacking from London to Brussels for the weekend.

Inspired by the ultra distance cycle races such as the Tour Divide, The Trans Am Bike Race or the Trans Continental Bike Race, I'd been pondering a bikepacking trip for a long time. But thinking I needed a specialist touring bike, I had put the idea on the shelf. Until, that is, I realised I was being misled by my own ignorance.

Previously, when picturing traditional cycle touring, I had imagined overladen bikes with panniers stuffed with everything but the kitchen sink. It looked painfully slow – and really hard work. But then, as I watched the bikepacking scene emerge, I saw that I had made a mistake. Instead of thinking I needed specialist panniers, or indeed a fancy new bike, I simply had to reassess what I *needed* to take with me on a cycle journey, as opposed to what I would *like* to take.

At one end of the extreme you have credit card touring. But bikepacking is a little more gentle and less expensive. There doesn't appear to be a hard and fast definition of what bikepacking entails, except it's a sort of mashup between mountain biking, long-distance cycle touring and camping. It's an opportunity to go off the beaten track on a gravel or mountain bike or take the back roads with your existing road bike. The key element is the 'less is more' approach.

The best bike is the one you already have. It doesn't need fancy parts, it just needs to be reliable enough to get you from A to B – in my case, from London to Brussels. For a two-day journey, you don't need much more than a saddlebag stuffed with a few essential tools and some spare clothing. You can ride in the same kit each day and if travelling with a friend, you can always share the toothpaste, etc.

So, after buying a couple of 12-litre saddlebags for our bikes and borrowing a mate's Garmin GPS, we set off from our home in southwest London, feeling like intrepid explorers going into the unknown. Of course, it would have been prudent to have read the instructions before we left, as we hadn't got to the bottom of the road before we realised we had no idea how to safely leave the city by bike.

IF YOU LIKE THE SOUND OF THIS, THEN TRY:

Arch to Arch

Extreme Twinning

Col Collecting

Regardless, what we enjoyed about it was the sense of adventure and, most importantly, being in control of our own destinies. And even though the weather initially bordered on biblical, with the rain lashing our faces as we rode towards the ferry, we were still smiling. It all added to the experience – and looking back, I wouldn't have wanted it any other way.

When we finally arrived in Brussels in time to catch the train back, we were totally converted. It may not have been as epic as the Trans Continental, but it was really good fun. We'd cycled for over 200 miles through three countries, drunk Belgian beer, eaten chocolates and crepes, survived a storm and two punctures, travelled by ferry, train and Eurostar and stayed in two hotels. And to think that I'd put off this journey simply because we didn't have a 'touring bike'.

A FEW EXAMPLES
- TO -
GET YOU STARTED

La Grande Traverse du Pays Basque, France

The GR247 Southern Woodlands Trail – a loop of 317 kilometres around Andalusia's Sierras de Cazorla, Segura y Las Villas Natural Park

The Tuscany Trail – a journey of 600 kilometres across Tuscany

Peak Bagging

CLIMB AS MANY PEAKS AS POSSIBLE

PREPARATION TIME
3 HOURS

ADVENTURE TIME
24 HOURS -10years

Moderate

1 2 **3** 4 5
DIFFICULTY

💡 CONCEPT

Peak bagging is the art of summiting as many peaks as possible which conform to a certain altitude or prominence. Not only is climbing mountains a great way to keep fit, but it can also give us purpose. It's not something to be taken too seriously, simply a lifetime bucket list that you can slowly but surely tick off as you go.

☑ RULES

1. The summit must be reached by foot.

2. Unless you're bagging a significant series of peaks that no one else has done, you don't need to keep proof. This is for your enjoyment only.

🧭 KIT

- Trail running shoes
- Map
- GPS device
- Running backpack
- Food and water
- Waterproof jacket
- Spare warm top
- Emergency space blanket
- Whistle

🐾 METHOD

When the ill-fated British climber George Mallory was asked why he wanted to climb Everest, he famously replied, 'Because it's there'. But for peak baggers, it's more than that. If you've not come across the term peak bagging, it essentially means trying to reach the summits of a collection of peaks – commonly referred to as a list. And ever since Sir Hugh Munro created his first list of 'Munros' in 1871, walkers, hikers and mountaineers have been inspired to come up with hundreds more.

At one extreme you have the 8,000-metre peaks, of which there are only fourteen and which only thirty people to date have achieved. With all of these peaks falling in the death zone, the point at which you need oxygen, this list is very much the preserve of elite mountaineers. And then at the other end, and much more accessible to your average adventurer but still demanding respect, are the 283 Scottish Munros, mountains over 915 metres. A few hardy souls will try to complete these in one calendar year, while most are happy to tick them off over a lifetime.

But perhaps the most famous example of peak bagging is climbing the highest peak

on each of the seven continents (see 7 in 7, page 206). First achieved in 1985 by American Dick Bass and written about in the book *Seven Summits* which he co-authored with Frank Wells,

TOP TIPS?

Try to make the last hill on your list a special one – and, ideally, one that has somewhere to celebrate near the bottom.

Start small and work your way up to bigger lists. Some lists can be done in a day, others will take years.

Remember that this is meant to be fun, so don't take it too seriously. It's not about ticking boxes, no matter how satisfying; rather, it's about creating journeys that will enrich your life. Therefore, choose a list that genuinely excites you, no matter how long it will take.

this notion has since captured the imagination of many, from wealthy businessman to retired rugby star. For many a wannabe peak bagger, the seed is sown on the summit of Mount Kilimanjaro, the highest point in Africa, and from there, it's all, well, basically uphill. One down, six more to go, including the daddy of peaks, Mount Everest!

Of course, it doesn't have to be all crampons and oxygen masks. If climbing at altitude ain't your thing – and let's be honest, it's not for everyone – there are events such as the National Three Peaks challenge in the UK to give you inspiration, where thousands of people every year aim to climb the highest point in Wales, England and Scotland in one continuous push.

But the great thing about peak bagging,

aside from the satisfaction of creating a bucket list, is that it takes you to places that you'd have perhaps otherwise avoided. So when you arrive in a new country and discover that by chance you're not far from its highest point, the pull is unbearable. It's not unknown for people to drive hundreds of miles out of their way into the middle of nowhere in order to bag a high point, simply because it's there and it would be silly not to.

Every list is created by someone, and there are more than 200 on peakbagger.com, an exhaustive resource for aspiring peak baggers, but there's no reason why you can't create your own. The UK has a name for just about every type of hill or mountaintop, from your Corbetts and Grahams to your Nuttalls and Marilyns. But in continental Europe, beside the Alpine 4,000ers, the Pyrenean 3,000ers and the high points of various countries, departments and regions, there are surprisingly few – offering a perfect opportunity to claim your own.

A great place to start are the national parks. They're a veritable playground for adventure athletes and a source of inspiration. Besides the numerous canyons, forests and coastlines to

IF YOU LIKE THE SOUND OF THIS, THEN TRY:

Peak to Peak

Sea to Summit

Castle to Keep

explore, each park will have a high point. With twenty-four national parks in Italy, fourteen in both Germany and Spain respectively, and six in France, you could be kept busy for many years.

The most important point to remember with peak bagging is not to be too ambitious. Mountains and hills, whatever their prominence, need to be respected. To begin, create a list of the ten highest points in your local area – which you might be able to turn into a Peak to Peak round (see page 114). And before you know it, your holidays will be mapped out for years to come.

A FEW EXAMPLES
- TO -
GET YOU STARTED

Bag the Top 50 summits by prominence in your country

Climb the highest point in each country in Europe

Climb the Volcanic Seven Summits

Climb the highest point in each national park

Extreme Twinning

CREATE A CYCLE OR RUNNING ROUTE BETWEEN YOUR LOCAL TOWN AND ITS TWIN

PREPARATION TIME
3 HOURS

ADVENTURE TIME
3 HOURS- 7 DAYS

 Moderate

 **4** DIFFICULTY

 ### CONCEPT

Twinning was a concept born at the end of the Second World War to forge links between countries divided by war. More often than not, the only people to benefit from these relationships are the town mayors and the council. But if you've ever been harbouring a desire to travel, why not create a time trial between your home town and its twin?

RULES

1. The route should avoid busy highways and as much as possible follow quiet roads.

2. Where possible, links should be created with the cycle clubs of the respective towns, to encourage more people to make the journey.

KIT

- Bike
- Helmet
- Bikepacking kit
- Bike shoes
- Food and water
- Gilet

METHOD

I'm not sure when the idea of Extreme Twinning first occurred to me. In one sense it's totally barmy. Yet in another, it has inspired me to create a plethora of routes between cities in Europe that sound fun to visit.

As I looked at the map, tracing my finger along the almost vertical route between my local town of Oloron-Sainte-Marie and its twin, Jaca of Spain, sitting just 80 kilometres south of me, I couldn't believe my luck. With this being my first Extreme Twinning experiment, I was quietly grateful that I didn't have to cycle to Peru. But there it was, a fabulous bicycle route that not only handrails the Arles Way, an alternative section of El Camino de Santiago and an equally attractive running option, but which also passes a nineteenth-century fortress and what was, in 1928, Europe's largest international rail station – both now abandoned. My only obstacle would be the hors catégorie, 28-kilometre climb up the Col du Somport. All I had to do now was persuade some friends to join me.

Until this point, I'd been puzzled by the concept of twinning. Despite having lived in a multitude of cities and towns around the world, many of which had been twinned with a random town somewhere miles away, I'd never once thought about visiting its twin. But this had now changed.

The first recorded twinning link was back in 1920, between Keighley in West Yorkshire and France's Poix du Nord. But it wasn't until after the Second World War that twinning became a formal practice, with the idea of forging links and encouraging reconciliation between countries divided by war. There was a further twinning boom at the advent of the European Economic Community (now the European Union), and then after 1989 and the fall of the Soviet Union.

✓

IF YOU LIKE THE SOUND OF THIS, THEN TRY:

Arch to Arch

Castle to Keep

Peak to Peak

Almost a century after the first twins were created, there are now well over 20,000 towns twinned with one another.

Most towns and cities are happy to be twinned with just one other town, while at the other end of the spectrum, cities such as Lima, the capital of Peru, are twinned with as many as twenty-nine cities around the world, surely a baffling number to remember.

Luckily, my local town of Oloron-Sainte-Marie in France gave me just one choice – Jaca. But as I made preparations for my inaugural ride, and simultaneously tried to find recruits to join

me, I couldn't help but see what other Extreme Twinning possibilities lay on my doorstep. Before I knew it, I'd plotted routes taking me all over Europe, some multiday bikepacking expeditions and others doable in one or two days.

As my research into Extreme Twinning continued, I realised I was missing a trick. If twinning is designed to forge relationships, then surely I should be trying to create a link between cycling clubs in my respective town and its twin. Suddenly, the pieces of the puzzle began to merge. It doesn't matter what nationality you are – we cyclists are bonded by

TOWNS WITH TWINS, BY COUNTRY

See twinning.org

France – 5,953

Spain – 807

Italy – 2,096

Germany – 6,092

UK – 1,998

Sweden – 1,361

A FEW EXAMPLES
- TO -
GET YOU STARTED

Paris (France) to Rome (Italy)

Manchester (UK) to Amsterdam (Netherlands)

Biarritz (France) to Cascais (Portugal)

Oloron-Sainte-Marie (France) to Jaca (Spain)

Berlin (Germany) to Budapest (Hungary)

Barcelona (Spain) to Bordeaux (France)

our love of two wheels and the pure joy that cycling gives us.

So, instead of ignoring that sign pointing to a twinned town somewhere in the world, embrace it! Find out where it is, create a route, contact the local cycle clubs in your respective towns and put a date in the diary. It takes only one person to create the spark for the fire to spread. Whether you choose to cycle or indeed run to your twin town, the moment you leave the border of your town and begin your journey to the other, you're forging a link that will stand forever.

Hut to Hut

TO RUN/MOUNTAIN BIKE BETWEEN REFUGES, MAKING THE HUT THE POINT OF THE VISIT

PREPARATION TIME
10 HOURS

ADVENTURE TIME
1-5 DAYS

No

1 2 3 **4** 5
DIFFICULTY

 ## CONCEPT

A fastpacking multiday mountain run between huts and refuges. Travel fast and light – saving weight by staying in refuges rather than carrying a tent.

RULES

1. Respect the rules of the huts, such as leaving muddy shoes in the entrance porch, not making noise after 11 p.m., etc.

2. Leave no trace. It's vitally important to not leave any litter behind.

KIT

- 20 litre backpack
- Sleeping bag liner
- Micro-towel
- Wash kit
- Trail running shoes
- Poles
- Food and water
- GPS watch

METHOD

'I'm afraid they didn't have any of the smaller rooms left,' I tell Zayne reluctantly after booking our final night's accommodation of our upcoming holiday. 'So we'll have to share a twelve-man bunk room. But on the upside, the views should be amazing…'

Now, this isn't your normal holiday. In preparation for running the Ultra Trail du Mont

✓

IF YOU LIKE THE SOUND OF THIS, THEN TRY:

Trail Time Travelling

Castle to Keep

Run the Bridges

60 Minutes

If travelling in July/August, reserve your accommodation in advance.

The majority of 'guarded' European refuges are open from late June to the end of September, but if they're on a prominent ski-touring route or near a ski station some will reopen again for the winter months.

If you're short of time, and want a taster of mountain hut life, find one that takes your fancy and create a two-day route to the hut and back.

Some national parks, particularly in the United States, require permits. Make sure you have one if necessary.

Blanc, I had asked my then girlfriend Zayne if she wanted to run the Tour du Mont Blanc with me. At over 100 miles and with a mind-boggling 10,000 metres of elevation, it's not something that you just slip into a conversation, let alone a holiday, without some planning. I'd also suggested fastpacking the route in five days and not the usual twelve – not what most couples do for their first romantic break together.

If you're not familiar with the term, fastpacking (sometimes referred to for speed hiking) is essentially a lightweight version of hiking. Rather than carry a heavy rucksack, you take a 10–20-litre pack with just the bare essentials. Rather than walk, you run. And on this occasion, rather than camp, you stay in mountain huts.

Also known as refuges, *rifugi*, *doma*, *hütten* or bothies, the humble mountain hut is a beacon of hope to many a hiker, runner and climber. They come in various shapes and sizes, and more often than not, you get to share this experience in a bunk room with as many as twenty people. There is your basic 'un-guarded' bothy with a bunk bed and a few logs for the open fire, to refuges that verge on the luxurious, with a restaurant, en suite accommodation and perhaps even a hot tub.

That said, the accommodation commonly borders on the basic, which also happens to be part of its charm. What makes many of the mountain huts so special is the fact that more often than not, there's no easy way to get there. Except by running, hiking or skiing.

When tackling a multiday run, whether it's around a mountain or point to point, the biggest hurdle is deciding how long to do it in. We broke our 100-mile adventure down into five 20-mile days, but we could have easily reduced it down to three. We then tried to find refuges en route that were situated at 20-mile intervals.

Carrying everything we needed in our small running packs, we set off from Chamonix on a warm day in late July. Both of us felt a shared sense of excitement, as neither of us had done anything like this before. And with no Wi-Fi or phone signal, we felt well and truly off the grid.

Running just shy of a marathon a day including 2,000 metres of ascent it is not for the faint of heart and, if you're new to long-distance running, probably not a good idea to do without some training. But if we wanted to arrive in good time at our refuge, we had no choice but to run the flat sections and power walk up the steep

A FEW EXAMPLES - TO - GET YOU STARTED

Le Tour du Canigou – French Pyrenees

Le Tour de Monte Rosa – the Alps

Haute Route (Chamonix to Zermatt) – the Alps

Traverse of the Jura – France and Switzerland

Grand Traversata delle Alpi – through the Italian Alps

bits. Once we reached the summit, we'd soak in the panoramic views before running down the other side of the mountain with childlike enthusiasm.

Depending upon your route and how remote you plan to go, there shouldn't be a need to carry a week's worth of food. Just make sure you pass the odd village or town where you can get supplies. Luckily, in our case, there was a stream or water fountain at almost every turn, so we were never short of water. And if you take the half-board option at the refuges, you won't need to worry about any of your meals. Many follow the custom of a communal dinner, where all the guests simultaneously sit down to eat a hearty carbohydrate-fuelled dinner, exchanging stories of their day in the mountains. It really is rather lovely.

Arriving back in Chamonix, five days and 100 miles later, although weary and somewhat dirty, we couldn't stop smiling. We'd just had the best holiday ever.

Perimeter Bicycling

CYCLE AROUND THE EDGES OF COUNTRIES AND STATES

 **PREPARATION TIME** 5-15 HOURS

 **ADVENTURE TIME** 5 HOURS- 100 DAYS

 No

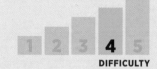 1 2 3 **4** 5 **DIFFICULTY**

 ## CONCEPT

Ernest Hemingway, the American novelist and journalist, once wrote, 'It is by riding a bicycle that you learn the contours of a country best, since you have to sweat up the hills and coast down them.' If you've ever ridden around the coast of an island, you'll know this to be true. Perimeter bicycling takes this concept one step further, encouraging us to cycle around a geographical entity, whether that be our local city, a lake, county or, indeed, our country.

RULES

1. In order for your record attempt to be ratified, you must join the Perimeter Bicycling Association of America (PBAA) and submit new routes for prior approval.

2. For a perimeter route to be accepted, a perimeter is defined as a 'defined geographical boundary of at least 50 miles or more', as defined by the PBAA.

KIT

- Bike
- Helmet
- Bikepacking kit
- Bike shoes
- GPS
- Map

🥾 METHOD

Having spent much of my life going around in circles, whether that be running around the block or my local park, or simply creating a route that brings me back to where I started, I'm surprised it took me so long to discover the world of perimeter bicycling. After all, I've both run and cycled around the perimeter of London and many other towns and parks. Surely, someone might have mentioned something.

Perimeter bicycling – or 'perimeter riding' as it's called in some circles – is essentially creating a circular route that traces 'a geographical boundary of 50 miles or more such as: towns, cities, lakes, counties, states or countries'. The definition is courtesy of the custodians of all perimeters, the Perimeter Bicycling Association of America (PBAA).) You could, of course, add islands and mountain ranges to this list.

Now, you may be thinking: 'Who on earth cycles around a country?' Believe me – there are a dedicated group of people from around the world who take perimeter bicycling very seriously. So much so, that if anyone harbours a plan on setting a world record, it needs to be 'recorded and officially verified' by the PBAA.

It's more than likely that you've not heard of this unusual cycling sport, even if you've already done a few perimeter rides yourself. But if you're looking for a bit of inspiration, your first port of call might be to read up about the Perimeter Queen, Joan Joesting-Mahoney. Although she passed away in 2014, this remarkable woman still holds the record for the most perimeters cycled and the most distinct perimeters, including cycling around Australia and twenty other countries in Europe – most of which she did on a fold-up bike she called Bike Friday.

Of course, unless you happen to be retired or homeless for a couple of weeks or months or years, it's easy to assume that cycling around a country is a time-consuming business and beyond your ability. But you'd be surprised what's possible; there are plenty of options that you can fit in around your weekends and holidays. All it takes is some imagination, a map and some time spent researching.

Depending upon how ambitious you are, this is something that might be done in one day – like cycling around Malta or the Isle of Wight. Or you may choose an option that takes several weeks, perhaps three to four, such as cycling around Portugal. But if you're looking to set a record or establish an official route, then you'll need to sign up to the PBAA. If someone's already done it, then you follow the pre-existing route. If they haven't, then it's up to you to make one up. Naturally, some would argue that signing up to an organisation to ratify your cycling journey is a bit of a waste of money. But I'd argue that it's nice to have some form of official recognition for your achievement.

✓

IF YOU LIKE THE SOUND OF THIS, THEN TRY:

Extreme Twinning

Boundaries Run

Bikepacking

It's actually surprisingly easy to create a perimeter route, and possibly the most accessible and easiest to organise is one around your city's metropolitan area. For a big one, this will certainly be 50 miles or more. A cursory glance of Google Maps will show the administrative boundary of your city, but with a bit of creative licence, you can ensure your route passes train stations, allowing friends and supporters to join you for parts of the journey.

Cycling around an island has to be one of the easiest perimeters to do. In fact, if you

employ the Day Flight Run strategy (see page 102), you can do this in the space of 24 hours or a weekend. And the chances of getting lost are minimal. For instance, you could fly to Malta on a Friday night, hire a bike, cycle the 100 kilometres or so around the island and be back home the following evening for tea and medals.

Whichever option you choose – lake, city, island or country – it puts a whole new spin on the concept of going around in circles.

A FEW EXAMPLES
- TO -
GET YOU STARTED

Cycle the 160-kilometre perimeter of Italy's Lake Como – see griante.com

Cycle Highway 1, the 1,340-kilometre perimeter of Iceland

Cycle the perimeter of the Isle of Wight

Cycle the perimeter of Malta

Race to Space

CLIMB THE EQUIVALENT HEIGHT OF SPACE ON FOOT OR BIKE

PREPARATION TIME
2 HOURS

ADVENTURE TIME
12+ MONTHS

No

1 2 3 4 **5**
DIFFICULTY

💡 CONCEPT

If you live in a city, then it's more than likely you hate hills. They hurt, they take your breath away and, generally speaking, they are something to be avoided. But, if you make a simple change of mindset and start looking up, there is a new adventure awaiting you. One that will make you stronger, faster and healthier. But to get there, you've got to go to space. Not figuratively, but metaphorically, by vertically running and cycling your way.

☑️ RULES

1. In order to complete this challenge, you must accumulate 100,000 metres or more of ascent.

2. There is no time limit, although it is still a race. The quicker, the better.

3. Any sporting activity counts: running, cycling, climbing – as long as it gets you closer to your target.

🧭 KIT

Running:
- GPS
- Running shoes
- Top
- Socks
- Shorts

Cycling
- Bike
- Helmet
- Shoes
- Glasses
- GPS

METHOD

I close my eyes and open them again. Yup, I'm not dreaming. They're still there, twinkling away like diamonds in the sky. Having left the city to live on the edge of an International Dark Sky Reserve, I look up at the stars and realise I've almost forgotten that there is a world above us, begging to be explored. If only I could …

It's now that the lightbulb goes on. According to perceived wisdom, and if the

TOP TIPS?

What goes up, must come down. Be careful when running the descents, as you only get one set of knees.

The key to tackling hills is consistency. The more you do it, the easier it becomes.

Karman line is accurate, outer space sits some 100 kilometres above Earth. And although most of us will agree with Captain Kirk that space is 'the final frontier', it's a place that sadly few of us will visit in this lifetime. But, I ask myself, what if I virtually focus my efforts on vertical gain rather than distance? Given a bit of creative licence, maybe I can reach space.

When I lived in London and was training for mountain marathons, I learned to become creative with my training – running up and down skyscrapers, taking the stairs in the Underground or doing hill reps. But since moving to the foothills of the French Pyrenees, I haven't been able to avoid the lumpy stuff. Quite naturally, I've become less concerned with the miles I covered and far more interested

A FEW EXAMPLES
- TO -
GET YOU STARTED

Do an Everesting challenge once every month for a year

Aim to become an Officer of the Ordre des Grand Cols, the title award for those who reach 100,000 metres

Accumulate 2,000 metres of elevation gain every week through a combination of one cycle ride of a minimum of 1,000 metres of ascent, and three or four runs totalling 1,000 metres of ascent

IF YOU LIKE THE SOUND OF THIS, THEN TRY:

Col Collecting

Peak Bagging

YoYo Peaks

Everesting

in how many metres or feet of elevation I can accumulate in my run or ride.

I decide to set myself goals of not finishing my run until I've gained 1,000 metres of climbing, or more. And thanks to the likes of Strava or MapMyRun, which encourages us with monthly challenges to get elevation into our training, it puts a whole new spin on how I train. More to the point, it actually starts to make my training sessions fun.

Now, it's no point pretending that accumulating 100,000 metres of vertical gain, the equivalent of twelve Everesting attempts, is easy (see page 138). It isn't. And it's not for those new to the endurance world. Which is why it sits here, as a Long-Term Burner. It doesn't need to be in one continuous push – that would break all but the strongest of us. Rather, you decide upon a time limit – anything from twelve months upwards. What's more, you could cleverly combine it with one of the other challenges in this book, like attempting to join the Ordre des Cols Durs, found in Col Collecting.

As the weeks pass and my accumulative total starts to grow, I find myself getting stronger and stronger. Little niggles that have plagued me over time have disappeared, I am less out of breath and I even start to sleep better. This is no longer just a challenge; it's quickly turning into a lifestyle choice.

In some weeks when short on time, I'll do a series of 30-minute bike rides, often squeezing 400 metres of ascent, or I'll grab my trainers and do hill reps outside my home, easily gaining 500 metres. And in other weeks, when researching this book by chasing cols or running vertical kilometres up mountains, I clock up well over 15,000 metres.

This simple change of mindset has given me new focus. And ultimately, restored my love of running and cycling. If you want to get high, Race to Space. Maybe it's not the final frontier after all.

7 in 7

TAKE ON A CHALLENGE IN MULTIPLES OF 7

PREPARATION TIME
4 HOURS

ADVENTURE TIME
7 HOURS– 7 MONTHS

Moderate

1 2 3 4 **5**
DIFFICULTY

 ## CONCEPT

If ever there were a number that had more connotations than any other, it's the number 7. From the Seven Hills of Rome to the Seven Seas, its place in history has huge meaning – it's mentioned in the Bible 735 times. Regardless of its apparent good fortune, the number 7 also makes a very neat number for the basis of a challenge – anything from 7 summits on 7 continents, to 7 marathons in 7 countries in 7 days. Using this simple formula, try to create your own 7 in 7 challenge.

✍ RULES

1. Refer to the challenges in the book.

◎ KIT

- See individual kit list for the relevant chapter.

METHOD

I've kept this chapter until last, not because it's necessarily the most difficult (although it could well be), but because it brings together all of the challenges in this book into one neat package. Think of it as a lifetime goal.

The 7 in 7 concept is not a new one. It's most commonly associated with tackling a challenge on each of the seven continents, whether that be running a marathon, summiting its highest point, or paddling its longest river. But it's also a number that has enormous biblical, historical and scientific meaning, from the Seven Deadly Sins and the Seven Wonders of the World to the seven colours of a rainbow or, at its simplest, the seven days of the week. It also happens to be the luckiest number for many people.

But if you have neither the time nor the resources to travel around the world, including a rather costly trip to Antarctica, there's no reason why you can't do something a little more local. Think countries, states, departments or even towns.

You can divide the 7s as you will, but for the purposes of this challenge I've created a simple formula to help you come up with a plan:

IF YOU LIKE THE SOUND OF THIS, THEN TRY:

60 Minutes

Peak Bagging

YoYo Peaks

aG x L

It looks a bit funny, but bear with me.

aG combines an activity with a geographical entity. For example, completing a marathon or triathlon or swimming a set distance across a col, mountain, desert, lake or river.

L is the Location. For example, a country, region, department, mountain range, valley or perhaps a city.

All you need to do now is figure out what to do. As is often the case with these sorts of challenges, something will click. An idea will spring to mind that will make you sit up with excitement.

For instance, if you live in Australia, you might decide to tackle Victoria's infamous

7 Peaks Ride in seven weeks, widely regarded as the ultimate Australian alpine challenge. Or you could ride the 7th stage from the past 7 editions of the Tour de France over the course of 7 days. Another option is to run a trail marathon in each of the seven national parks of Austria over the course of seven months. There are endless ways to spin the number 7.

In numerology, those who walk the Life Path number 7 are referred to as seekers or thinkers. They're people who love to solve puzzles but they simultaneously see infinite possibilities. So, don't be afraid to dream big and be bold. This book is just a guide, a template for you to get outside and challenge yourself. What you do is totally up to you. Just make sure you tell us all about it!

A FEW EXAMPLES
- TO -
GET YOU STARTED

Run the 7 Hills of Rome in 7 hours – conveniently this has an elevation of 770 feet

Tackle the Brevet des 7 Cols in the Mercantour National Park in 7 days

Ride the 7th stage of the past 7 editions of the Tour de France over the course of 7 days

Run 7 trail marathons in all 7 National Parks of Austria over 7 days

Resources

MIDWEEK MADNESS

60 MINUTES

- For a comprehensive list of commemorative plaques for your country, go to openplaques.org

- English Heritage (english-heritage.org.uk) have helpfully created a GPS-enabled Blue Plaques App for your smartphone. Not only does it provide some guided routes, but it allows you to quickly identify any Blue Plaques close by.

HIDDEN WATERS

- Paul Talling, *London's Lost Rivers*, Random House Books, 2011.

- Tockner, Klement, Uehlinger, U., and Robinson, Christopher T., *Rivers of Europe*, Academic Press, 2009.

RACE THE COMMUTE

- Most cities have a travel website that allows you to plan your journeys, but an excellent universal tool is rome2rio.com

- Paris transport: www.ratp.fr/en/

- London transport: tfl.gov.uk/plan-a-journey/

- Although this doesn't strictly follow the rules of this challenge, if you've a spare 24hrs, you might want to take on the Tube Challenge (thetubechallenge.com), and attempt to visit every London Underground station (all 270) in the shortest amount of time possible. The current Guinness World Record stands at 15 hours 45 minutes and 38 seconds. A similar challenge exists in New York City – rapidtransitchallenge.com

RACE THE FUNICULAR

- funimag.com – a web magazine about funiculars. Includes a database of all the funiculars in Switzerland.

- Search for 'list of funicular railways'.

RUN THE BRIDGES

- The best way to plot a route crossing the bridges in your city is to use an online mapping tool, such as Strava, Ride with GPS or MapMyRun.

VERTICAL KILOMETRE

- A simple starting point for finding vertical kilometres is to search for any mountains higher than 1000m above sea level, which if you're near the sea would also tick off a Sea to Summit challenge.

- If you don't have any summits higher than 1000m, then you'll need to create a route incorporating enough hills to bring you up to 1000m. But the idea is to do it in as short amount of time as possible.

- Grouse Grind challenge: https://www.grousemountain.com/grousegrind/faq

FIVE TO NINE

- Humphreys, Alastair, *MicroAdventures*, William Collins, 2014.

URBAN TRI

- Search online for 'bicycle sharing schemes'.

- The European Cyclists Federation provides some history behind bike sharing schemes in Europe: https://ecf.com/

WACKY WEEKENDS

MONOPOLY MARATHONS

- To learn more about all things Monopoly, go to http://monopoly.wikia.com

- Search online for 'List of licensed and localized editions of Monopoly' to see if your country or town has its own board.

WILD AT HEART

- The ÖTILLÖ is the original SwimRun race and the one that inspired Tobias and his wife Zayne, when they completed it in 2014. There are a number of SwimRun races around Europe that you can set your sights. otilloswimrun.com

- For a list of international SwimRun events that might provide inspiration for planning your own SwimRun, visit swimrunfrance.fr

EVERESTING

- everesting.io – an online calculator that helps to work out how many repetitions of a segment you need to do to reach the height of Everest.

- everesting.cc – the home of all things Everesting and where you'll find the Hall of Fame and what climbs have already been Everested.

- https://www.grousemountain.com/grousegrind/faq – for information about the Grouse Grind.

YOYO PEAKS

- Feles du Grand Colombier – http://www.felesducolombier.fr

- Club des Cingles de Mont Ventoux: www.clubcinglesventoux.org/en/

- Les Barons du Soulour: http://baronsdusoulor.monsite-orange.fr

- Il Brevetto del Grappa in Italy (10 ascents by road and an eleventh on an MTB): altopianobike.com/notizie/ultime-notizie/il-brevetto-del-grappa.html

RACE THE SUN

- timeanddate.com/sun – gives the exact time for sunrise and sunset wherever you are in the world.

CASTLE TO KEEP

- A 954km route through Germany passing 100 castles: http://www.nrw-tourism.com/a-100-schloesser-route

- Search online for 'lists of castles'.

LONG-TERM BURNERS

PEAK BAGGING

- peakbagger.com – provides tons of lists, worldwide, for aspiring peak baggers.
- hill-bagging.co.uk
- peaklist.org – lists over 10,000 mountains worldwide.

COL COLLECTING

- thecolcollective.com – an inspiring resource of videos and information about how to tackle some of the greatest climbs in the world.
- cols-cyclisme.com
- cyclingcols.com
- bigcycling.eu
- climbbybike.com
- centcols.org – Home of the Club des Cents Cols.
- www.aukweb.net/ocd/ – UK site for the Ordre des Cols Durs.
- https://uctistes.wordpress.com/about/ordre-des-cols-durs/ – Union des CycloTouristes Toulousains – the home of the French club.

SOURCE TO SEA

- www.rhinecycleroute.eu – provides information on the Rhine Cycle Route, AKA EuroVelo 15.
- http://www.danube.travel/ – information about the Danube that will help you plan your trip.
- http://bicyclegermany.com/elbe.html – information about the Elbe River Cycle Route.

ARCH TO ARCH

- naturalarches.org – a great source of information for finding natural arches around the world.

EXTREME TWINNING

- Search for 'twin towns' or 'sister cities' for lists of twinned towns.
- twinning.org – provides information on history of twinning.
- Wikipedia is a great source of information for finding out if your town is twinned with another.
- Use websites like RidewithGPS or Strava to create a route between the two towns. Create a start point and a finish point, and let the mapping tool plan the rest.

BIKEPACKING

- bikepacking.com – a brilliant resource and source of inspiration for planning your bikepacking adventure.
- bikepacker.net – another great website packed with interviews, reviews and reports from the bikepacking scene.

HUT TO HUT

- List of French refuges: www.gites-refuges.com (in French).
- The Club Alpino Italiano provides a list of all their refuges by area www.cai.it (in English, French and Italian).
- Mountain Bothies Association – www.mountainbothies.org.uk
- www.irunfar.com

PERIMETER BICYCLING

- http://www.perimeterbicycling.com – The Perimeter Bicycling Association of America.

USEFUL WEBSITES

- HardasTrails.com – Tobias's blog and where a lot of the information in the book can be found.
- Ordnance Survey in the UK: https://www.ordnancesurvey.co.uk/osmaps/ – an excellent online mapping tool that will help you to plan your adventures in the UK.
- Strava (strava.com) has an excellent 'route planner' that will select a route based on popularity – saving you a lot of time in the process.
- viewranger.com has an app that allows you to download local maps to your phone from over 20 countries. For some countries, such as the UK and France, they offer a modest annual digital subscription service that allows you access to your respective country's maps.

FURTHER READING

Benson, Jen and Sim, *Wild Running:150 Great Adventures on the Trails and Fells of Britain*, Wild Things Publishing, 2014.

Brotheron, Lyle, *The Ultimate Navigation Manual*, Collins, 2011.

Clayton, Roy & Turnbull, Ronald, *The Welsh Three Thousand Foot Challenges: A guide for walkers and hill runners, 2nd Edition*, Grey Stone Books, 2010.

Gatty, Harold, *Finding Your Way Without Map or Compass*, Dover Publications, 2003.

Gooley, Tristan, *The Natural Explorer, Understanding your landscape*, Sceptre, 2013.

Gooley, Tristan, *The Walker's Guide to Outdoor Clues and Signs*, Sceptre, 2015.

Humphreys, Alastair, *Grand Adventures*, William Collins, 2016.

Thomas, Clive, *GPS for Walkers: An introduction to GPS, digital maps and geocaching*, Pathfinder Guides, 6th Edition, 2013.

Turnbull, Ronald, *Lakeland Mountain Challenges: A Guide for Walkers and Fellrunners*, Grey Stone Books; 2nd edition, 2010.

Turnbull, Ronald, *The Book of the Bivvy*, Cicerone Press, 2003.

Turnbull, Ronald, *Three Peaks, Ten Tors: And Other Challenging Walks in the UK*, Cicerone Press, 2007.

Smith, Phoebe, *The Book of the Bothy*, Cicerone Press, 2015.

Warren, Simon, *100 Greatest Cycling Climbs: A Road Cyclist's Guide to Britain's Hills*, Frances Lincoln, 2010.

ACKNOWLEDGEMENTS

It is often said that writing a book is a labour of love. Well, one thing is certain – it is not possible without the support of your family and your friends. Not only has my wife twice had to hold the fort, while I hide away in my study, fingers tapping away on the keyboard of my computer, but she's also been my sidekick and inspiration for many of the adventures in this book.

However, I also need to thank my wonderful friends and co-conspirators, whether they come from my running club, the Clapham Chasers, or those I've met in races and on adventures. It's amazing how little snippets of conversation can often spark an idea.

There's one thing to have an idea for a book of this style, but without photographs, it's sometimes impossible to bring it to life. When I first met James Carnegie at a press event in 2011, I not only made friends with a kindred spirit, but found someone who shared my enthusiasm for wacky ideas. Thank you James for your patience and inspiration.

Huge thanks should also go to my editor Lucy Warburton and the team at Aurum Press, Richard Green and Jessica Axe, for believing in me (again) and once more turning my ideas into the beautiful book you're now holding in your hands.

I also need to thank the following people and companies for helping me to bring this book together: Adam Marcinowicz, Matthew Hearne, Matt Buckley, British Airways Highlife Magazine, Jersey Tourism, Salomon, Inov8, dhb, and Wiggle. I would also like to thank the Haute Pyrenees Tourist Board for providing me with an epic playground in which to test many of these ideas, with special mention going to Celine Ringeval of the Valle de Gaves.